THE NEW IDEA
IN
EDUCATION

EXPLORATION SERIES IN EDUCATION
Under the Advisory Editorship of John Guy Fowlkes

HARPER & ROW, PUBLISHERS

NEW YORK, EVANSTON, AND LONDON

THE NEW IDEA IN EDUCATION

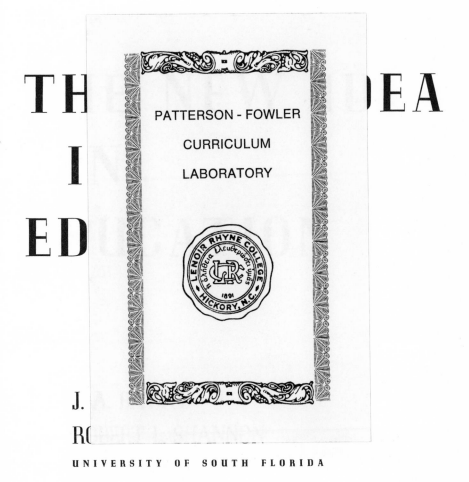

J.
ROBERT SHANNON

UNIVERSITY OF SOUTH FLORIDA

THE NEW IDEA IN EDUCATION
Copyright © 1968 by J. A. Battle and Robert L. Shannon

LIBRARY OF CONGRESS CATALOG CARD NUMBER: 68-25317

Contents

UNIT III   By What Means Do We Teach?

UNIT IV   The Process of Becoming

Editor's Introduction

Time was when scholarship was measured by how large a volume of facts had been assimilated by an individual and the skill displayed in the parading of the storehouse of "knowledge." For those who held the concept of learning just presented, it is not surprising that the concept of a teacher was that of a person who listened to the recitation of sums or equally monotonous performances such as naming the presidents of the United States and giving the dates during which they held office.

Happily there seems to be a daily realization that neither scholarship nor teaching as defined above are likely to meet the social needs of the kind of society that prevails today and seems likely to develop during the immediate years ahead. For life today, learning must be recognized as the process of finding out by and for oneself. In light of this concept of learning, it seems clear that teaching at its best is the process of stimulating and advising learners to learn. Assuming that the latter definitions or concepts of learning and teaching are valid, it seems clear that traditional forms of organization of educational institutions governing entrance policies and practices, along with the classification and measurement of the academic achievement of students, demand sharply different practices concerning the classification and evaluation of student achievement, or more appropriately, student development.

The very title of the volume hereby presented, consisting of a carefully selected group of writings by various authors is positive proof that there is a new idea in education or, indeed, that there are diverse forms, facets, or aspects of the new idea in education. It is my considered judgment that both laymen and professionals who are truly concerned with, and who participate in, the planning and/or support and/or the evaluation of what goes on in educational institutions will find this work enlightening, stimulating, and interesting.

JOHN GUY FOWLKES

Foreword

To be a teacher is to be a creative artist in the medium of human lives, to be able to quicken into action the intellectual life of the child. It is therefore crucial that the teacher not only be sensitive to the child and his needs but also that he possess a body of knowledge and have an intellectual life of his own. Under the present system, very few teachers have learned to live such a life, to look at their society as it really exists, or to become sensitive to the political, moral, and social issues that agonize the world. Nor have they learned to become aware of the quality of their experience or that of the culture that surrounds them. Their tastes and attitudes are approximately the same as those of the rest of society, educated or uneducated. The reason is that their college courses are either trivial or academic—the products and the stock-in-trade of academic experts, not those of fresh insight and new thinking by students and teachers working together at common tasks. Academic studies leave the heart untouched, and therefore do not affect the mind. A true college for teachers would break down the wall between the reality of life as it is lived in the world and the artificial, institutionalized life created by educators inside the colleges. The campus would become a staging-ground for expeditions into the world, a place where students could learn how to use the world as an educational instrument.

HAROLD TAYLOR

From the June 27, 1967, issue of LOOK Magazine. Copyright 1967 by Cowles Communications, Inc.

THE NEW IDEA
IN
EDUCATION

The Viewpoint

The New Idea in Education has been prepared for the student who wants to consider teaching as a profession and for the layman who, as a citizen in our American democracy, needs to learn about some of the important issues in education.

To introduce the student to the profession of teaching and to the issues in education it is not necessary nor desirable for him to begin at once to learn the actual art and science of teaching. This can probably be best begun after the student has completed at least two years at a liberal arts college. It is important, however, that a student begin as soon as possible to think about education from the standpoint of a citizen and, if he is so inclined and has the qualifications, from the standpoint of a career.

Erasmus was a wise man but was he correct in saying that teaching is the noblest of occupations? The editors of this book of readings believe that his statement is true, but with this qualification: Teaching is noble only when the students learn about noble ideas and ideals and when what is learned is relevant to the problems of the students' world. Teaching of any other sort is only an exercise in futility.

For teaching to be noble the students must learn to think for themselves. Young people have been told so often by parents, teachers, and politicians that they must learn to think for themselves that it is generally believed that they do. Yet, students who try to act on this preachment sometimes get in trouble at home, at school, and at large.

But the American schools have been more successful than schools of almost any other nation in teaching pupils to think. That it has not been more successful has been due partly to the lazy habit of human beings to copy the past rather than to think for themselves on how to make the present better. Thomas Jefferson criticized those who are addicted to this habit in the following words:

> They pretended to praise and encourage education, but it was to be the education of our ancestors. We were to look backwards, not forwards, for improvements. . . . But the endeavors to enlighten them on the fate which awaits their present course of life, to induce them to exercise their reason, follow its dictates, and change their pursuits

1

with the change of circumstances, have powerful obstacles to encounter; they are combatted by the habits of their bodies, prejudice of
their minds, ignorance, pride, and the influence of interested and crafty
individuals among them, who feel themselves something in the present order of things, and fear to become nothing in any other. These
persons inculcate a sanctimonious reverence for the customs of their
ancestors; that whatsoever they did, must be done through all time;
that reason is a false guide, and to advance under its counsel, in their
physical, moral, or political condition, is perilous innovation; that their
duty is to remain as their Creator made them, ignorance being safety,
and knowledge full of danger; in short my friends, among them is
seen the action and counteraction of good sense and bigotry. . . .*

It is not important whether the substance of one's education be new
or old if it is arrived at by the process of thinking. Josiah Royce has said,
"Thinking is like loving and dying. Each of us must do it for himself."
Thinking is the method of education and it results from the pupil's own
unique experiences and not from a set of beliefs handed to him in a neatly
wrapped package exactly like that given to all potential learners. So to each
individual the content of education is always new.

An ever-present problem facing educators in America, as in every nation, is "to play it safe" with the public by teaching only for the perpetua-
tion of the present society rather than to so teach that their students can
develop a better society. The wrath of those who feel threatened by
change is terrible to incur, but change is inevitable and students must be
taught to control it rather than to be controlled by it. Those who oppose
change do sometimes perform an important function because they slow
up change which is made solely for the sake of change. But they also tend
to keep the school from dealing honestly with the relevant problems of
the day. As a result the school seems to discuss problems of past ages
more than current problems. While this may offer some temporary
safety for teachers, it leaves the society as a whole open to destruction.

Today, as Elmo Roper has said, "Only a patient and informed mind,
only a mind which literally never stops growing is prepared to contribute
to modern democratic society. Never has there been so much to learn,
unlearn, relearn." To believe as truth without examination another man's
thoughts, whether a classroom lecturer or a textbook author, is a parody
on education. There can be no true education unless there is an intellectual
involvement on the part of the student as an individual. And it needs to
be emphasized that this involvement does not have to be a physical one.

* John Dewey, ed., *The Living Thoughts of Thomas Jefferson*, New York, Fawcett Publications, 1964, pp. 117–118.

As much thinking can result from a lecture as from a visit to a local electrical power plant.

It is not nearly as important for a pupil to possess a great amount of knowledge as a sense of wonder. If he has the latter, knowledge will follow. The passage of Terence which states that nothing human is foreign should apply with equal force to the teacher and to the teacher's influence on the pupil. An insatiable curiosity is the hallmark of both the teacher and the student. This curiosity, which should create a union between theory and experience, is indispensable if learning is to take place.

J. A. BATTLE

The New Idea in Education

A devoted follower of the late Pope John XXIII, the Rt. Rev. John M. Oesterreicher, stated in describing the Pope's inspiration to the Second Vatican Ecumenical Council: "The Council is to open windows." Furthermore, he said he believed that the Council must not content itself "with decrying the undeniable wickedness of man; rather it must remind him of his native dignity as a person and his supernatural calling as a child of God."

Pope John had said in December of 1962 that one of the most important missions of the papacy is in "giving this ancient and eternal doctrine a relevancy corresponding to the conditions of our era." After his death, six months later, Xavier Rynne wrote of the Pope: "He was faithful to the past but devoted to the present and he was wise enough to know that nothing from the past can really be preserved unless it is made meaningful here and now."

The person who perhaps is more responsible than any other one man for the new scientific world we live in today is Francis Bacon, who died in 1626. Bacon fervently believed that if scientists were allowed to develop fully and exploit their studies that man would gain control of his destiny while on earth. He defined the true scientist as a person of both compassion and understanding who realizes that knowledge without charity has the deadliness of a serpent's venom. In his *Advancement of Learning* Bacon clearly expressed his concern for more than knowledge. He said there is a necessity for knowledge to be applied for the benefit of humankind. He especially insisted, "We must gather from the whole store of things such as make most for the uses of life." A Bacon biographer, Loren Eiseley, has recently written: " 'For the uses of life,' we might well reiterate, for so he intended, and this is why his green continent lies beyond us still in time. Five little words have shut us, with all our knowledge, from its shores—five words uttered by a man in the dawn of science, and by us overlooked."*

"For the uses of life" does not mean to do only the immediate and

---

* Loren Eiseley, *Francis Bacon and the Modern Dilemma*, Lincoln, Nebr., University of Nebraska Press, 1962, p. 65.

4

practical. For life to be sustained at an intellectual and spiritual level it needs, of course, more than bread. To climb mountains or to explore space could well be "for the uses of life." One might ask, "Why does man need to climb mountains or explore space?" The classic answer to such a question was given by the British mountain climber, George Mallory, who later died on Mount Everest. When asked why he wanted to climb Everest, he replied, "Because it is there."

When anyone today actually tries to build an educational program "for the uses of life," except possibly in science and technology, he is likely to be overwhelmed by the hordes of proponents of tradition, folk-lore, and mythology. While seldom is modern technology put to the use of "the good life," most educational programs in the humanities and the social sciences have been formulated on the premise that the realistic present had best be forgotten. Bertrand Russell put it well when he said, "It is because modern education is so seldom inspired by a great hope that it so seldom achieves a great result. The wish to preserve the past rather than the hope of creating the future dominates the mind of those who control the teaching of the young."

The modern world is shackled today by an old idea in education which is not a poor idea because it is old but because it simply is not adequate for the last third of the twentieth century. The old idea in education is a simple one: "thinking" and "agreeing with the teacher" are considered to be identical and education is thought of as a ritualistic form of mental exercise. Until science and technology made some changes possible, there were almost no educational programs that did not follow this pattern. It dominated education not only in the old world, but also in the new world, which copied the educational practices of the old. Pupils listen to instructors relate so-called facts of the past or the present or they read them in books, and then these "facts" are transcribed or parroted back. Furthermore, there is an arbitrarily set period of time for pupils to "learn" subject matter and if they do so, they are given enough points to qualify as "educated men." Incidentally, "men" until this century usually meant the male sex, for in the past centuries this was "too serious" and "too intellectual" an exercise for women.

The old idea in education provides almost no opportunity for the pupils to ask questions and to discover truths through their own firsthand experiences. To do so is a hindrance to getting good grades and grades instead of significant knowledge are the real goals of this system. Seldom do pupils have the opportunity to feel the bite of new ideas. Instead of challenge, adventure, and excitement the system offers sterility and dull-ness. The would-be scholar finds himself living the theme of the old hymn, "How Tedious and Tasteless Are the Hours."

In his book *Who Killed Society?* Cleveland Amory writes of Mrs. Edward C. Barry, a railroad lineman's daughter who served for more than a quarter of a century as editor and "almost sole arbiter of a strange and mysterious little black book—the *Social Register*." Amory says, "Mrs. Barry, in contrast to so many others who have spent their lives propping up something they have really never understood, was not only a simple person but a modest one to boot." Many of the persons who have either given their lives or their spare time to "propping up" American education have also never really understood it. And like Mrs. Barry their stock in trade is mythology, although their ultimate authority is not Burke's *Peerage, Baronetage, and Knightage* but instead the old idea in education. This doctrine which resists the idea that social change and quality can be made compatible usually has no more basis in the realities of today than Mrs. Barry's *Social Register*. When it, too, can find no "past" for a subject, it manufactures one and whether manufactured or real it is its past with which it is most enamoured. This old idea in education is one which is akin to the philosophy of the late Mrs. "Mimi Bird" King of Houston who, Amory says, "refused to read any modern newspapers at all. Instead she kept newspapers of twenty years ago—and these she reread every day."

It should be emphasized before defining the new idea in education that it is the antithesis of the narrow "presentism" which is the hallmark of a shallow and popular cult of "practical men" of every age. Such "presentism" may be worse than staying in the old familiar ruts. Neither novelty nor tradition alone contains the solutions to the problems of the space age. But if man is to live significantly, or even continue to survive, there must be an end to the rule of dogma—whether it is fortified by the grand traditions of the past or the novelty halo of the present—with its impediments to inquiry, debate, and thinking. With such impediments removed, it will be understood that education is not a matter of semantics.

One of the characters in Boris Pasternak's *Doctor Zhivago* says, "Perhaps ignorance was the trouble? An educated man can see through walls, he knows everything in advance, while the rest of us are like people in a dark wood. We only miss our hats when our heads have been chopped off." Yet being designated as an "educated man" by an educational system does not necessarily mean being an "educated man" who can "see through walls." Many an "educated man" has not even become aware of the wall which he is supposed to be able to "see through." If one is going to be effective in the twentieth century he must get more than a pseudo-education.

If it will be of any comfort to the traditionalists we will mention here that the new idea in education is in the tradition of ancient Greece in that among its most important goals are truth, goodness, and beauty. It would only add that what the ancient Greeks thought of as truth is not necessarily truth today. The student who believes in this new philosophy of education is so concerned with truth and goodness that he is not as likely to confuse change with progress as those who have been educated in subject material that is primarily irrelevant to life and who have been subjected to a learning process almost entirely dependent on memorization. A student believing in the new idea in education so values beauty that he opposes the vulgarity of the times based on materialistic values alone, such as "get-rich-quick" real estate subdivision developments in which all the trees are bulldozed, leaving only telephone poles for shade and esthetic enjoyment. Unlike so many who buy and see the developers' homes built on streets with names such as "oak," "cypress," or "birch," he not only sees the irony in such designations but he wants people so educated that those following such a barbaric and age-old type of practice will either have to become civilized or go out of business and preferably the former.

An educational philosophy is greatly needed today which will serve as an intermediary between the almost unyielding past and the compelling future. The new idea in education could be this philosophy. It is possible that the task of mediation will not be so difficult if it is realized that the new idea in education is not actually new in terms of years but only in the degree of acceptance. This "new idea" has been known to a few intellectually superior persons for at least twenty-four centuries and probably much longer. It was known by Socrates, who was born about 470 years before Jesus Christ, and it was known by Christ. Socrates was in agreement with an important facet of this viewpoint when he said, "The unexamined life is not worth living." Christ was in agreement when he stated, "The Sabbath was made for man, and not man for the Sabbath" and when He took the child from the periphery of life and made him central by teaching "Whoever receives one such child in my name receives me." These statements are a basis for many of the principles underlying the new idea in education—both its substance and its process. When these principles are followed in an educational program each student is shown the respect due every human being, is given the opportunity to learn what is relevant to his life today as an individual and as a member of society, and is encouraged to become so deeply involved in a self-educational process that he is able to gain a true desire to continue learning.

"The educated man," according to Carl Van Doren, "is neither scared by novelty nor bored with it." Yet until a relatively few years ago, when science started making so many new and startling discoveries, most teachers taught as if all new ideas were educationally unsound. Today there are some teachers who make the opposite mistake of acting as if only the new is sound. In general, however, change in attitude and thinking about education has been tediously slow. Because of its willingness to experiment, only science is really out of the middle ages. Although there are many scholars and teachers in all disciplines today who protest against rote, insignificant learning, not enough act on the sentiment of Johann Goethe when he said, "A teacher who can arouse a feeling for one single good action, for one single good poem, accomplishes more than he who fills our memory with rows on rows of natural objects, classified with name and form." If "quality education" in America is to get out of the "talking stage" and become a reality, the scientific method must be understood, adopted, and humanized by scholars and teachers of the humanities and social sciences. But this is not enough, for students and teachers of the natural sciences, too, must be partners in this enterprise and refuse to be apologists for the old order who think foolish Goethe's contention that "if you treat an individual as he is, he stays as he is . . . but if you treat him as he ought to be, he will become what he ought to be."

Professor Alexander D. Alexandrov, an internationally esteemed mathematician and the Rector of Leningrad University, recently made a strong criticism of the entire Soviet system of higher education. In his article, published in the newspaper of the Young Communist League, he wrote against the Communist control over the minds of men with its deadening effect upon the creative achievements of the individual. Professor Alexandrov stated: "The student is not a vessel to be filled but a lamp to be lighted." He deprecatingly pointed out that the educational system of Soviet Russia rewards knowledge over ability, memorizing by rote over critical thinking, and routine attendance at lectures over solitary research in the laboratory. Priscilla Johnson, former North American Newspaper Alliance correspondent in Moscow and at the United Nations in New York and currently with the Russian Research Center at Harvard University, has said that in the article "Alexandrov struck a blow at nearly all of Soviet higher education, which stands as a monument to the official apprehension as to where independent thinking by the lone scholar may lead."

James Thurber was ridiculing a too typical example of the old idea in education when he wrote:

> Ohio State was a land grant university and therefore studied the tactics of the Civil War even though the World War was going on at the time. At 11 o'clock each morning thousands of freshmen and

sophomores used to deploy over the campus, moodily creeping up on the old chemistry building. It was good training for the kind of warfare that was waged at Shiloh but it had no connection with what was going on in Europe. Some people used to think there was German money behind it, but they didn't dare say so or they'd have been thrown in jail as German spies. It was a period of muddy thought and marked, I believe, the decline of higher education in the Middle West.*

It is no wonder that Alfred North Whitehead, the great English mathematician and philosopher, would comment on university education as follows: ". . . I have been much struck by the paralysis of thought induced in pupils by the aimless accumulation of precise knowledge, inert and unutilized." **

The old idea in education was well established long before it was suspected that there would be a behavioral science concerned with learning called psychology, which emphasized motivation—that within the individual which stimulates his action. And it was established before the American dream began to be realized. American scholars and statesmen, in fact, have been the leading advocates of the new education, which opposes the habits of the old world that shackle the spirit of man. Such statesmen as Benjamin Franklin, Thomas Jefferson, and Woodrow Wilson all helped in refining this new idea. It was natural that a pioneer people should have leaders who promoted the new idea in education with its desire to enhance the worth and dignity of each individual, to break the lock step in education which offered the same fare to each recipient, and to give the opportunity for learning to all according to their capabilities. It was also natural that the idea that "education is a voyage and not a harbor" would have more appeal in a pioneer country than in the old world with its rigid social and economic structures.

Franklin, who was a rare combination of scientist and philosopher—and who was a better scientist for being a philosopher and a better philosopher for being a scientist—contributed to the new idea in education by seeking a synthesis between the theoretical and the practical. Jefferson encouraged others to stop following without reason "respectable authority and tradition." He wrote to Dr. Joseph Priestley:

> What an effort my dear sir, of bigotry in politics and religion have we gone through! The barbarians really flattered themselves, they should be able to bring back the times of vandalism, when ignorance

* James Thurber, *The Thurber Carnival*, New York, Dell, 1945, p. 259.
** Alfred North Whitehead, *The Aims of Education and Other Essays*, New York, Macmillan, 1964, p. 46.

put everything into the hands of power and priestcraft. All advances in science were proscribed as innovations. They pretended to praise and encourage education, but it was to be the education of our ancestors. We were to look backwards, not forwards, for improvement. . . .*

Woodrow Wilson gave expression to both the dynamic and individualistic features of the new idea in education when he said, "The mind is not a prolix gut to be stuffed" and "the use of a university is to make young gentlemen as unlike their fathers as possible."

Blind acceptance or rejection of the new or the old is not the way the educated mind works. Yet while no idea should be accepted or rejected on the basis of its age, it is true that almost every new idea, discovery, or invention made by man, no matter what its merits, has had to counteract unevaluated, traditional thinking to get accepted. This has happened just as often in other areas as in education. The six most disturbing things in the world have been described as nightmares, mosquitoes, forgotten appointments, income-tax notices, other people's successes, and new ideas. Whether this is a fair analysis or not, it is certain that new ideas do create disturbances. Critics laughed at the steamboat, "Fulton's Folly," and at the purchase of Alaska, "Seward's Icebox." They hooted at early automobile drivers and said that if the Lord had intended for man to fly, He would have given him wings. Meanwhile, the men who were making new discoveries and inventions continued undaunted to try to find what they considered the better way, although their attempts were more often failures than successes. They did not believe in the new just because it was new, but because they thought it was better. They kept on searching with faith in themselves and in the future and turned deaf ears to the cynics and pessimists who in every generation try to hide behind the past to keep from facing the future.

While we should not adopt the new just because it is new, we also must not fool ourselves into believing that we are finding a true and safe haven when we retreat to the old. The unexamined old is no truer and no safer than the unexamined new. Those who are continually exhorting Americans to return to the old idea in education, with its lack of faith in the intellectual potentialities of many, are actually demonstrating a lack of faith in the American dream. The American dream is based on change and change that offers more qualitative opportunities to more people. As the late President Kennedy insisted so clearly: "It is those who are satisfied with things as they are . . . who are in reality selling America short. It is they who have lost their faith in America."

* John Dewey, ed., *The Living Thoughts of Thomas Jefferson*, New York, Fawcett, 1964, p. 117.

If the American educational program is to be successful, it must be based on the American idea of life. This idea does not make a distinction between the voice of the people and the voice of quality, but it does make a distinction between the voice of the hereditary elite and the voice of God. It does encompass the suspicion that the voice of such an elite, once in power, usually becomes the voice of the devil. On the positive side, it goes even further than Aristotle who exclaimed that the least bad form of practical government is democracy. It shows a more affirmative faith in democracy, provided that this democracy is undergirded with an educated citizenry. And it must be constantly emphasized that an "educated citizenry" means not one that "parrots" the most facts but one that has learned to relate facts in a significant way to life. To develop an "educated citizenry" it is not as necessary to develop "photographic memory" as the ability to think. Such a citizenry must have some of what William James called the primary quality of artistic intelligence—the knack of similar associations, the faculty (or incurable habit) of putting flint and steel together and getting fire, of putting two people or images or ideas together and getting a sudden depth of focus, a parallel, a deepening of meaning and value. What the advocates of the old idea in education need to learn is that it is not the specifics of the old traditions that are always immortal, as important as they may be, but instead in every new age it is the spirit of man as a thinker that must not be destroyed.

Followers of the new idea in education remember George Santayana's barbed wisdom: "Those who cannot remember the past are condemned to repeat it." They try to understand the past to keep from repeating it while others just repeat it without understanding it. It does not seem likely that a proponent of the old idea in education would view the universe with the same respect and humility as it is viewed by one who believes in the new idea. "Understanding" the universe is not as difficult a task for the follower of the old idea. To him truths are valid in all times and all places and to "understand" them one simply seeks out the proper authority, who will tell him the final answers. The new idea in education, on the other hand, is an open-minded and an open-ended viewpoint. Its thesis is that the universe is so intricate that the search for the truth can never end as long as man has an intellect. This truth can sometimes be discovered after meticulous, objective inquiry but when one solution to a problem is found, it almost invariably points to new problems which need solutions. The realization that final answers about the universe are so seldom discovered and that any answers are revealed only after much intense searching should give one respect for the complex universe in which he lives. Moreover, when he finds that the more he learns the more he needs to know in depth and breadth, he can hardly keep from being profoundly humble.

A humility which is an outgrowth of such knowledge was expressed by Dr. Tsung-Dao Lee. In October of 1957, while he was at the Institute for Advanced Study at Princeton, New Jersey, he and his colleague, Chen Ning Yang, were awarded the Nobel Prize in physics for "their penetrating research into the laws of parity which has led to major discoveries concerning the elementary particles." In his laureate address Dr. Lee said, ". . . there is in Chinese a saying 'Jump as you may, it is not possible to jump out of the Buddha's palm.' In our search for knowledge, we may be making rapid progress. But we must remember that even at the bottom of the Buddha's finger we are still very far from absolute truth." Thus man has to continue to try, to dare, and to seek.

The failure of education to face the realities of the present has helped to produce a neurotic and shallow society. Although William Whyte's *The Organization Man* may exaggerate the situation, it nevertheless describes an all too prevalent type in modern life: the man who sacrifices "selfhood" on the personality market for "advancement," who voices a code of values quite different from the one he lives. He may express a deprecating attitude toward the present and talk with nostalgia of the virtues of the past while worshipping today's god, "success," and striving only for a future in which he envisions his name at the top of the line and staff chart. He is akin to the modern official whom James Reston, *The New York Times* columnist, described as "confounded at every turn by the hangover of political habits and outworn institutions" while he is no longer "nourished by ancient faiths" on which they were founded.

Historians relate how over the centuries each new conqueror who founded a dynasty along the Nile River worshipped the sun. Yet because of the sun it was almost impossible to survive a short walking distance away from the warm, brown waters of the river. So it was strange that man would worship the death-dealing sun instead of the life-giving river. But this is not unique in man's history, for throughout the history of civilization man has usually paid homage to an idea in education which has hindered rather than helped him to gain the insight he has needed to cope with himself and his world.

There is no doubt that the most significant development in Western society in the last several centuries is the transformation of its civilization through science. We are told that the possibilities for the "good life" through the utilization of science are almost limitless. This could be correct if science is guided by the finest of man's moral and intellectual values. To believe that science, like a headless monster, should dictate to man as if he is its servant is an unscientific notion and unworthy of the being described by the Scriptures as "a little lower than the angels." But to guide science intelligently man must have not only specialized knowledge, but also a true liberal education which shows him the relationships between all branches of intellectual endeavor and makes him more humane. The old idea of education, which conceals or sometimes distorts the facts of life, is not sufficient for this day.

Arnold Toynbee has written that "this is the first age since the dawn of history in which mankind has dared to believe it practicable to make the benefits of civilization available to the human race." If education is to be the decisive factor in bringing on this age of which Toynbee writes, then it cannot be guided by clichés which have caused too many of its products to be either apathetic or extremely rebellious and the society they have helped to create to be too stolid, static, and synthetic in almost every area except science and technology. In this latter part of the twentieth century, the "educated man" must no longer be afraid "to stick out his neck." He can no longer be concerned with returning to the "safe" past or with perpetuating society for today and tomorrow. To improve the present society, man's ideas must be oriented to this age of the scientist rather than to the age of the "medicine man." Yet with this orientation, it is vitally important that man be made central instead of the cold hard facts of science. Only then will he be able to "see through walls." Alfred North Whitehead succinctly stated the need: "Ideas won't keep. Something must be done about them."

Just as Socrates brought philosophy down from Mount Olympus, there is a need today for scholars and teachers to bring the new idea in education from the minds of the few into the practice of the many. If this were done, its impact might be such that the nineteenth-century ideas of Karl Marx could not compete and would become only of historical interest to the world. In this potentially most promising and most dangerous of ages, it is now time to do more than write or talk about the new idea in education, which reason and experience tell us is better. It is now time to unleash this new idea which could lead us to that green continent so clearly seen by Francis Bacon in the dawn of science. And what have we to lose when now we cannot even dimly see the shore?

What Is Teaching?

Everyone has been exposed to teaching, and most people believe they know what is meant by the term teaching. However, because teaching is such a common and complex occurrence, it is extremely important for each person to study carefully what is involved in the teaching task when it successfully promotes learning. The readings in this unit provide many possible answers to the question, "What is teaching?" Use them to reexamine your personal concept of teaching and attempt to formulate refined understandings which reflect an extension of your present perspectives. It is frequently stated that an essential element in education is to create circumstances in which persons will reexamine what they believe. This must be a quality of your behavior as you contemplate the question, "What is teaching?"

What do you think?

Think of a time when you were taught something. What makes you think you were taught? What do you think you learned? Describe the teaching which promoted that learning.

A teacher often teaches that which he did not intend to teach. Why? What is the significance of this for teachers and teaching?

Under what conditions do you learn?

Is talking teaching? If so, when?

Think of the best teacher you ever had. Why do you think of that teacher as "best"?

Authentic Teachers

Discussing a common school problem, a parent recently asked me, "How is it that some teachers are able to control their classes with a very light rein, and have no disciplinary troubles, while others must shout and plead and threaten and still get nowhere with the trouble-makers?"

I don't think the answer has much to do with teaching techniques or even experience, beyond a certain degree. I think it has almost everything to do with the "authenticity" of the teacher.

Notice I do not say "authority," but "authenticity." For genuine authority, which is more than a matter of official position and the ability to reward or punish, comes out of the depths of the personality. It has a realness, a presence, an aura, that can impress and influence even a six-year-old.

A person is either himself or not himself; is either rooted in his existence, or is a fabrication; has either found his humanhood or is still playing with masks and roles and status symbols. And nobody is more aware of this difference (although unconsciously) than a child. Only an authentic person can evoke a good response in the core of the other person. Only a person is resonant to person.

Knowledge is not enough. Technique is not enough. Mere experience is not enough. This is the mystery at the heart of the teaching process; and the same mystery is at the heart of the healing process. Each is an art, more than a science or a skill—and the art is at bottom the ability to "tune in to the other's wavelength."

And this ability is not possessed by those who have failed to come to terms with their own individuated person, no matter what other talents they possess. Until they have liberated themselves (not completely, but mostly) from what is artificial and unauthentic within themselves, they cannot communicate with, counsel, or control others.

The few teachers who meant the most to me in my school life were not necessarily those who knew the most, but those who gave out the fullness of themselves; who confronted me face to face, as it were, with

Sydney J. Harris, "Authentic Teachers," *Phi Delta Kappan, April,* 1964, back cover.

a humanhood that awoke and lured my own small and trembling soul and called me to take hold of my own existence with my two hands.

Such persons, of course, are extremely rare, and they are worth more than we can ever pay them. It should be the prime task of a good society to recruit and develop these personalities for safeguarding our children's futures; and our failure to do so is our most monstrous sin of omission.

"A society in which the young people have lost their boldness and sense of adventure and zest for exploration and risk-taking and their capacity for dedication is headed for the history books."

—JOHN W. GARDNER

What Is Teaching?

Teaching is a process of arranging conditions under which the learner changes his ways consciously in the direction of his own goals.

There are three words in this definition that are key words. They are: (1) conditions, (2) consciously, and (3) goals.

When we look, first at this process of arranging conditions for learning, we must never forget that the first and most effective teacher is the learner himself. In education every learner is his own teacher. In training, the trainee is never his own trainer. The rat in the maze, learning to take the right-hand path beacuse the left-hand one leads to an electric shock, is being trained by the electricity and by the psychologist, not by his own conditions. He (Mr. Rat) doesn't know what the conditions are. All he knows about this process is that he does not want to get hurt.

Much of human learning is incidental. There is no teaching involved because the learner's ways are not being changed *consciously*. To have real teaching, therefore, the learner must know what is going on. He must know the score from the outset.

This means, furthermore, that the learning and teaching process is directed toward the learner's own goals. If a learner's ways are being changed in the direction of goals he does not understand and accept, he is merely being trained, not taught.

The professional teacher reaches the heights of his craft when his pupils become their own best teachers, consciously setting up conditions for changing their ways in the direction of their own goals. The good teacher is always trying to work himself out of his teaching role by getting the learners to assume that role for themselves.

This statement was written by Dr. Benjamin for use in *The New Idea in Education.*

Dr. Benjamin is an eminent educator, writer, and editor. Probably his best-known work is *The Saber-Tooth Curriculum.*

J. A. BATTLE

What Is Good Teaching?

At a meeting concerned with planning the curriculum of a new university, the University of South Florida, I asked a distinguished visiting professor from the University of Chicago the attributes of a good teacher. He replied that there are only two essentials: to be "an interesting person" and to be "well educated." Few could argue with these two attributes, but they are so general that they do not go much beyond Mammy Yokum's framed motto hanging over her mantlepiece which announces that "Good is better than evil because it is nicer."

The real problem concerns the particulars as to what is meant by "an interesting person" and "well-educated." From the tone of his answer I surmised that the Chicago professor would agree with Robert Hutchins about the lack of importance of methodology. (He was, in fact, a great admirer of Hutchins.) Nevertheless, I can certainly agree with both of his essentials as far as they go. Yet the first requisite of a good teacher—that he not be boring—must be qualified as to techniques used to accomplish this end. Some highly paid comedians are interesting persons to their audiences but the philosophy, psychology, and sociology which some of them practice are not the procedures of the good teacher. Also, a teacher can be interesting in a classroom by depending on cheap efforts such as off-color stories, picking on awkward members of the class, or just being a smart aleck in general. Yet the need for such techniques is proof that he is a poor rather than a good teacher. A good teacher does not "jazz up" his presentations so that the jazz either outshines or counteracts the central theme of the subject he is supposed to be teaching. The best teacher may have a fine sense of humor, but he keeps interest alive through his knowledge of his students and the world. Such knowledge enables the teacher to generate excitement by dwelling on the spirit and quality of intellectual experiences. We all need to remember, as Clifton Fadiman has said, "School is still the main, sometimes the only chart to the most glamorous of all Treasure Islands—the child's own mind."

Being an "interesting person" and a "well-educated person" are parts of the same fabric and must be especially so for the teacher. Although

20

each is a part of the other, neither knowledge of process nor knowledge of subject matter alone makes the good teacher. But both of these requisites were combined in the "1961 Teacher of the Year" of whom her principal remarked: "She gives her students the kind of salt that makes them thirsty for knowledge." A teacher can create such a desire to learn only when process and subject matter are well interrelated. Education then becomes an exciting adventure of learning what is relevant. The soundest method cannot make innocuous subject matter interesting to intelligent people. But a synthesis of sound method and sound subject-matter can provide the kind "of salt that makes them thirsty for knowledge."

Teaching what is relevant is teaching what is concerned with the world of today. This does not mean, however, that yesterday and tomorrow are forgotten. It only means that if one does not live for today one does not live at all because, obviously, yesterday is gone and tomorrow is not here. Yet the good teacher does use the learning of both yesterday and today in preparing his students for tomorrow. For instance, in teaching what is relevant to the world of today he needs to maintain the spirit of the Platonic tradition in which truth, beauty, and goodness are paramount.

One can be interesting even in using the lecture technique of teaching alone if he can utilize brevity, point (or relevance), and wit. I have elaborated on relevance and wit but brevity is also important if the student preparing to become a teacher is to be an interesting talker. And incidentally, talking and teaching are not necessarily synonymous. Teaching candidates might remember that the greatest ministers of the churches of our nation spend almost a whole week preparing for one sermon or lecture, and most of them are careful not to take more than twenty minutes to deliver it. This emphasizes not only the importance of brevity in speech but also the need for much study.

Probably the surest and best way for a teacher to make a class interesting is simply to get the students so involved in their own educational process that they put so much intelligence and vigor in their work that it becomes a part of them. The question, then, is how to get them so involved? We will try to answer it briefly by saying that the subject the students are studying must be clearly shown as having personal importance to them and the teacher must make possible for them some real experiences which are of significance.

This brings us to the second requisite of the Chicago professor: to be a good teacher one must be "well educated." One might write a book on what it means to be "well educated." Certainly one can't depend upon a standard dictionary definition of education: "Act or process of

educating; discipline of mind or character through study or instruction."
Even for a short definition this one could be improved upon. One might
get a better concept of "education" from Ambrose Bierce's *The Devil's
Dictionary* in which he defines it as "That which discloses to the wise
and disguises from the foolish their lack of understanding." But from a
more positive and more direct point of view, education can be defined
as active intellectual inquiry, the pursuit of truth through the medium of
knowledge and ideas. Education as the transmission of knowledge may
be a dull affair, but active inquiry and critical thinking must necessarily
be an interesting enterprise. But if the teacher believes that knowledge
and intelligence or memorization and education are the same, then the
students' educational fare is almost sure to be dull.

If a teacher's knowledge gives him a false pride which causes him to
act toward his students in a patronizing and condescending manner, he
is neither interesting nor well educated. The good teacher respects his
students. He needs to take the attitude that he may know more than
the student about the subject he is teaching but the student knows more
than he about other subjects. He has to have the humbleness suggested
in Will Rogers' statement: "We all are ignorant, just on different subjects." A graduate student at the University of Southern California challenged me on this point: "Give me an example of a situation in which
one of my junior college students might know more than I would know
as the teacher." The only answer that came immediately to mind was
the old one, "He would certainly know better than you where his shoe
was pinching him."

If a teacher has become cynical through his "education," he has not
really been educated. In teaching as a cynic he fails in his important
responsibility to help the young minds entrusted to his care to find a
worthwhile system of ideals and values. Constant negativism is bad, for
a truly good teacher can see both sides of a problem. The good teacher,
however, is not an "on-the-other-hand" type of person who can never
make choices between right and wrong. Such a person may be so bland
that he is almost totally uninteresting, but more important he is actually
amoral. If Alfred North Whitehead's belief is correct, that "the essence
of education is that it be religious," then he is not educated at all. So
the Chicago professor's definition of "education" would have to be understood before one could evaluate his statement concerning the attribute
of the good teacher.

The public needs to be reminded that a professor is a person who
professes something, but in doing so he is the opposite of a totalitarian
"brain-washer." Socrates was neither the first nor the last teacher to
suffer because he persisted in "professing" ideas that other people ab-

horred. The good teacher must reserve the privilege of sometimes disagreeing with popular opinion, and he must give his students the same right to disagree with him. Just as he expects a toleration for his disagreement he must allow it in others. It was in this spirit that a president of Harvard University made the statement, "There is a Harvard man on the right side and the wrong side of every important issue."

R. F. Bayles and F. L. Strodtbeck have demonstrated through research that members of small groups accustomed to working together establish a "pecking order"; one of the group is believed to know best or to be most competent to decide, and the other members of the group surrender the exercise of their own free will to him. In the long run such groups prove to be most inefficient because all except the person at the top of the "pecking order" stop thinking. The good teacher must create a healthy environment for agreement and disagreement. If this is done, thought will have a climate in which it can grow. The good teacher, therefore, encourages students to object when they feel they have relevant evidence. The good teacher must likewise instruct students so they realize that they have an obligation "to be thoughtful in objection, not be showoffs or thoughtless obstructionists," to use the words of Robert H. Beck. Only if there is an opportunity for students to make their own choices— and their own mistakes—through logic rather than emotion can they be taught to think. Certainly "spoon-feeding" them the answers through lectures or by just looking them up in the back of the book is more likely to create dogmatists instead of thinkers.

My own choice of the good teacher would not include a person whose education consisted of the memorization of inert facts and who was indoctrinated rather than having learned to think for himself. The educated man must accumulate accurate information, but he must spend even more time in learning to learn, for the world is always changing and old solutions seldom apply to new situations. To be an educated person today in these changing times a person must not only have this desire to keep on learning but have developed the aptitude of constantly making choices based on his ideals and values as these are related to each new situation. The good teacher then is never satisfied with his teaching. He must be like the writer described by William Faulkner. When asked "Is a writer ever satisfied?" he replied, "If he is he should cut his throat and quit."

JOHN DEWEY

The Function of the Teacher

His Need of Abundant Knowledge

The practically important question concerns the conditions under which the teacher can really be the intellectual leader of a social group. The first condition goes back to his own intellectual preparation in subject matter. This should be abundant to the point of overflow. It must be much wider than the ground laid out in textbook or in any fixed plan for teaching a lesson. It must cover collateral points, so that the teacher can take advantage of unexpected questions or unanticipated incidents. It must be accompanied by a genuine enthusiasm for the subject that will communicate itself contagiously to pupils.

Some of the reasons why the teacher should have an excess supply of information and understanding are too obvious to need mention. The central reason is possibly not always recognized. The teacher must have his mind free to observe the mental responses and movements of the student members of the recitation-group. The problem of the pupils is found in subject matter; the problem of teachers is what the minds of pupils are doing with this subject matter. Unless the teacher's mind has mastered the subject matter in advance, unless it is thoroughly at home in it, using it unconsciously without the need of express thought, he will not be free to give full time and attention to observation and interpretation of the pupils' intellectual reactions. The teacher must be alive to all forms of bodily expression of mental condition—puzzlement, boredom, mastery, the dawn of an idea, feigned attention, tendency to show off, to dominate discussion because of egotism, etc.—as well as sensitive to the meaning of all expression in words. He must be aware not only of their meaning, but of their meaning as indicative of the state of mind of the pupil, his degree of observation and comprehension.

His Need of Technical, Professional Knowledge

The fact that the teacher has to be a student of the pupil's mind, as the latter is a student of subject matter in various fields, accounts for the

From *How We Think*, by John Dewey, © 1933, pp. 274–277. Reprinted by permission of D. C. Heath and Company.

teacher's need for technical knowledge as well as for knowledge in the subjects taught. By "technical knowledge" is here meant professional knowledge. Why should a teacher have acquaintance with psychology, history of education, the methods found helpful by others in teaching various subjects? For two main reasons: the one reason is that he may be equipped to note what would otherwise go unheeded in the responses of the students and may quickly and correctly interpret what pupils do and say; the other reason is that he may be ready to give proper aid when needed because of his knowledge of procedures that others have found useful.

Unfortunately this professional knowledge is sometimes treated, not as a guide and tool in personal observation and judgment—which it essentially is—but as a set of fixed rules of procedure in action. When a teacher finds such theoretical knowledge coming between him and his own common-sense judgment of a situation, the wise thing is to follow his own judgment—making sure, of course, that it is an enlightened insight. For unless the professional information enlightens his own perception of the situation and what to do about it, it becomes either a purely mechanical device or else a load of undigested material.

Finally the teacher, in order to be a leader, must make special preparation for particular lessons. Otherwise the only alternatives will be either aimless drift or else sticking literally to the text. Flexibility, ability to take advantage of unexpected incidents and questions, depends upon the teacher's coming to the subject with freshness and fullness of interest and knowledge. There are questions that he should ask before the recitation commences. What do the minds of pupils bring to the topic from their previous experience and study? How can I help them make connections? What need, even if unrecognized by them, will furnish a leverage by which to move their minds in the desired direction? What uses and applications will clarify the subject and fix it in their minds? How can the topic be individualized; that is, how shall it be treated so that each one will have something distinctive to contribute while the subject is also adapted to the special deficiencies and particular tastes of each one?

ROBERT L. SHANNON

What Did You Learn Today?

Mother's solicitous comment was well introduced when she routinely inquired of her child, "What did you learn in school today, dear?" Perhaps Mother's question was sincere. Perhaps it was no more than a greeting. Nevertheless, it overlooks the basic nature of the learning process. Teachers frequently commit the same blunder, but in the teacher's case it is a needless professional misunderstanding. Too often a teacher will say, "Well, boys and girls, let's review what we have learned today." What a ridiculous instructional procedure. Such a practice is full of false assumptions and violates the fundamental principle that *Learning is a process not a product.* Review is an important quality in the learning process, but it is probably a miracle if what is reviewed is the same as that which each individual has learned, and if it is, there is no reason to review. Review of the day might serve to clarify some misunderstandings or be an extension of the learning process. Also, Mother might more accurately say, "Tell me some of the things you did today as you participated in the learning process." The essential point here is that persons must be cognizant of this principle as they examine the consequences of learning experiences. The entire instructional procedure acquires proper dimension if teachers remember that *learning is a process—not a product.*

When does one learn? The answer to this is obvious, but the significance of the relatively simple answer is tragically neglected in fashioning learning experiences. *Learning occurs in any situation to which the individual attaches significance.* Most persons can understand the importance of this principle by recalling some "behind the barn" experiences they have had. These are frequently significant situations, and learners are never quite the same as a result. Because they were significant, the learners learned. They realized changes in behavior and revised certain qualities of living as a consequence. Not all persons choose a barn as the environment, but they do identify a locale for such situations and the result

Robert L. Shannon, "What Did You Learn Today?" *Childhood Education,* May, 1967, 499–501. Reprinted by permission of Robert L. Shannon and the Association for Childhood Education International, 3615 Wisconsin Avenue, N.W., Washington, D.C. Copyright © 1967 by the Association.

certainly promotes further learning. Teachers must establish significant situations—significant according to learner's perceptions. This principle is the basis for motivation.

School programs can be made valuable for learning if it is remembered that *learning is an intensely personal affair.* If acquisition of knowledge is an objective, the curriculum must personalize the knowledge. Occasionally a teacher attempts to fulfill this principle by saying "You'd better get this 'cause you'll need it in life." Whether we accept it or not, it is a fact that learners decide for themselves what knowledge they need and want. Too often students discover that the knowledge they need consists of how to obtain an "A" grade because this enables a fulfillment of other goals the structure requires. So they *learn* how to get an "A," and if this means temporary retention of fragmental knowledge, they will approach the fragments with this motive. But it must be remembered that the personalized learning was to identify the route to "A." When knowledge is successfully structured around personal needs, it is learned. Because of its personal nature, learning cannot be artificially manipulated.

Perhaps the most discouraging consideration in teaching is that *people change their beliefs slowly.* Each teacher believes he knows so much that he is convinced would be great for all others to know. Sometimes, the teacher feels that getting a group of learners in a room, telling them what he knows and then having the learners tell him what he told them will result in their changing their beliefs because of the new knowledge he has "given" them. Sadly for the teacher, these learners just don't get it. He has neglected to remember that people change their beliefs slowly. A requirement for learning is that learners must experience a place in which mind changing is feasible for them, and that they be given sufficient time (and there is no magic schedule) to change their beliefs according to their personal perceptions of the new knowledge.

Occasionally teachers resort to threat to promote learning. The result is temporary acquisition of whatever the threat requires and prompt rejection of the materials as soon as the threat is removed. Although many studies have demonstrated the uselessness of threat for promoting learning, many teachers deliberately design a complex system of threats as basic to their instructional practice. Unfortunately, some teachers are not cognizant of the threatening circumstances they promote. *Sensitivity to the negative consequences of threat* as related to education is extremely important when considering the learning process.

Self-acceptance is a significant influence on learning. When persons are able to accept themselves as worthwhile individuals—when they positively accept themselves—their approach to behavior is favorably influenced. Conversely, persons who do not accept themselves as worthwhile, those who feel negatively about themselves, are adversely influenced by the feeling when they face many learning situations. Promoting positive self-acceptance becomes an imperative role of the school because of the significant relationship the self-concept has to perceiving the learning situations.

Challenge is a fundamental element in learning. One is challenged when there is a possibility of both success and failure. There is obviously no challenge in trying to throw a basketball through a basket if the ball is too large to go through the hoop. Only the possibility of failure exists. Conversely, dropping tennis balls through a waist high basketball goal is no challenge either. When the learners can perceive a learning situation as a personal challenge, the probability is great that they will significantly extend their understandings of the ideas being pursued. Arranging challenging situations (as the learner perceives challenge) becomes a basic responsibility in teaching.

Active involvement of the learner is probably the most important single factor in the learning process. Participating in identification of questions to which he wants answers, experiencing an environment in which he actively seeks answers to these questions, and identifying further questions based on his new knowledge is the continuing sequence in learning. When students are required to obtain the teacher's answers to the teacher's questions, there is no longer a genuine pupil participation and learning of a positive sort ceases. Promoting student participation of this type becomes a primary task in any instructional endeavor. Jerome Bruner, in his book, *On Knowing*, effectively emphasizes the importance of students participating in their own education: "Whether one speaks to mathematicians, or physicists, or historians, one encounters repeatedly an expression of faith in the powerful effects that come from permitting the student to put things together for himself, to be his own discoverer." Active student involvement is indispensable to learning.

Although there is much that is not known about learning, the foregoing principles are vital to creating conditions favorable for education. Teachers who neglect these principles "keep school." Those who apply these principles "promote learning."

Any study of teaching properly includes a look at the learners and how they learn. "What did you learn today?" Answers to the question are found by examining the quality of the learning situations persons experience. This quality is measured by analyzing the extent to which these basic principles are present in the environment for learning which the teacher establishes.

JERROLD K. FOOTLICK

The Revolution in Learning

The date was Oct. 4, 1957. The Soviet Union rocketed into space the first man-made satellite—Sputnik. This was truly a shot heard round the world and nowhere was the explosion more stunning than in American schools.

Why not us first, Americans wondered, and for all the speeches of politicians and explanations of scientists it was clear that the United States was not the undisputed leader in learning that most Americans had blithely assumed.

The search began for a reason—some say a scapegoat—and the American education system was a likely target. In articles, books, and speeches, the nation was told that its schools were lazy and out-of-date. Invidious comparisons were made to foreign systems.

From this shock the nation recovered—but not without upheaval. In less than a decade, more major changes have been made in the curriculum of American schools than in any comparable period of history. Outstanding scholars, such as Jerrold R. Zacharias, the Massachusetts Institute of Technology physicist, have turned their attention to the public schools. Private foundations, such as the Carnegie Corporation with farsighted and inspirational leadership from John W. Gardner, have supported experiments. The Federal Government has provided money that no other institution could have. A new breed of leadership has emerged in the public-school system.

Most of the changes are still in progress. They will build on themselves into the foreseeable future. And change begets change; as each step forward is taken, adjustments are required in the structure to keep pace. If high school students are learning more advanced chemistry, for example, must not the colleges advance their programs?

The date was Oct. 4, 1957, and in many minds the changes can be traced to that moment of Sputnik. In a way, they can be. For not until the shock of Sputnik had the country's attention been so focused on its educational system.

Jerrold K. Footlick, "The Revolution in Learning," in *Education, A New Era*, Newsbook, published by the *National Observer*, 1966, pp. 10–15.

But the evidence is clear, in retrospect, that Sputnik did not set off these changes. The system had always moved at a gradual and continuing pace. Over the years, English scholars, for instance, had debated new methods of analyzing the language—what has been called "the new linguistics"—to free it from the out-dated influence of Latin. That debate continues. But now, thanks to forces like the College Entrance Examination Board, the Modern Language Association, the National Council of Teachers of English, and the Federal Government, the pace quickens.

During the twentieth century, the whole concept of American public education has undergone major change. From the older theories that children should be taught as much as possible of the available knowledge about any subject, a new world of "progressive education" rose to prominence in the 1920s and 1930s.

Based on then-new studies of the psychology of learning and educational sociology, the "progressive" system held that teaching should center on the readiness of the child to learn and the social goals of the schools. Strict studies of the academic disciplines were considered less important. One pertinent illustration is an influential pair of reports issued in 1942 by the National Committee on Science Teaching of the Department of Science of the National Education Association. The titles speak for themselves: *Science Teaching for Better Living* and *Redirecting Science Teaching in the Light of Personal-Social Needs*.

Now the pendulum has swung back to the academic disciplines. In part this is because "progressive education" has been blamed for many of the school's presumed weaknesses. However much this may be true, the better reasons are more positive.

For one thing an even newer psychology of learning now holds that a child is never too young to learn, so long as he is taught in a way that respects his intelligence and fits his world. The theme was sounded by Professor Jerome S. Bruner of Harvard University: "Any subject can be taught effectively in some intellectually honest form to any child at any stage of development." The Montessori schools are one example of how this can be done; another is Miss Mason's School at Princeton, N.J., where mathematical concepts are swallowed up by eager children of 3, 4, and 5 years old.

And it has now become clear that there is so much to be learned, that the process of learning enough to be a scientist or a professional is so long and difficult anyway, that a child must be ready to begin serious learning sooner. He must and can be made ready. Educators realize that the academic subjects are the best way to organize and expand man's knowledge.

Such deep and far-reaching changes take time. Yet no one can deny the increased tempo of the last decade. That is why knowledgeable people speak of the "revolution in learning."

It is not easy to label a precise starting point for a revolution. To assume that the American Revolution began at Lexington Green on April 19, 1775, would be to dismiss the Stamp Act, the fiery speeches of Patrick Henry, the Boston Tea Party, and countless other events. But one thing about revolutions is that they often begin with wars. And it is fair to say, perhaps, that the one in education did too—the Second World War.

The recruiting of millions of young men revealed how badly they had been taught in such fields as science and mathematics. They had not been taught enough; and their learning was almost incredibly out of touch with the scientific advances of the twentieth century.

This realization awakened scholars, especially the scientists and mathematicians, to their responsibility for past weaknesses and future needs. But by then, the scientists had already climbed out of their ivory towers, not to touch the public schools but to aid the war effort. The Manhattan Project, a consortium of scientific prowess that developed the atomic bomb, is perhaps the best-known example; the list of similar contributions is almost endless.

The academic community could never be the same after that. Previously the scholars hadn't seemed to care what went on in the public schools—now they did. With the end of the war came the age of automation and computerization, putting another premium on advanced knowledge. Science and the scientists were having an unprecedented effect on society. Society was having its effect on the scientists.

"It was largely a matter of social conscience, I believe, that motivated us to school work," says Professor Zacharias. "As Scientists, we seek evidence before we try to create order, or orderliness, and we do not expect, nor even hope for, complete proof. Nevertheless, uncompleted as our theories may be, they all enjoy, in a sense, the benefits of due process of law. Dogmatism cannot enter, and unsupported demagoguery has a tough time with us. A Hitler or a McCarthy could not survive in a society which demands evidence which can be subjected to examination, to re-examination, to doubt, to question, to cross-examination. It may be this lesson that gives us a missionary zeal."

This zeal poured forth in the 1950s. Mathematics was off to the earliest start, with the University of Illinois program under Professor Max Beberman, in 1951, and in the following years more than a dozen similar projects in the "new math" followed. The first major science program grew out of the Physical Science Study Committee (PSSC), organized by Professor Zacharias at MIT in 1956 with the co-operation of university professors, high-school teachers, industrial scientists, and technical specialists.

PSSC did a great deal more than provide a "new physics" course. It showed how scholars and teachers could work together. It pioneered the use of such modern instructional devices as films. It showed how a complete instructional program could be packaged. And it emphasized that the mere passing of so many facts was not enough; the basic concepts of the subject had to be grasped.

In all these things Professor Zacharias was a driving and creative force. He is, in the words of one educational leader, "a man who sees a solution on an appropriate scale to the problem." The problems may have been awesome, but his solutions were just as impressive.

One of the most significant of these solutions was the formation of Educational Services, Inc. (ESI), a private, nonprofit organization in Watertown, Mass., which grew out of PSSC. With its own staff of scholars, scientists, teachers, and specialists in various teaching media, and the co-operation of others around the country, ESI has been responsible perhaps for more educational innovation than any other single group. It has centered on one site movements in physics, chemistry, biology, mathematics, the social sciences, international education, and a variety of other projects.

But these things take money, and ESI has no formal governmental connection to get any. Similarly most experimenters in new learning have limited budgets. To the rescue here came private foundations and the Federal Government.

John W. Gardner, who is now Secretary of Health, Education, and Welfare, is a psychologist by training and a professor by vocation who in 1956 became president of the Carnegie Corporation. "The right man in the right place at the right time," comments one colleague. Mr. Gardner once wrote a book called *The Pursuit of Excellence,* and he drove all his own creative and inspirational talents and a huge chunk of Carnegie money toward that goal.

For all its millions, the Carnegie Corporation (it is really a foundation but Andrew Carnegie formed several and needed different names) lacks the capital of such giants as the Ford Foundation. Under Mr. Gardner, the corporation became noted for its careful planting of "seed grants" to help start some of the most enterprising of new educational programs. In most cases, after they showed promise, other foundations and the Federal Government injected the funds to help them continue.

It was the Carnegie Corporation, for example, that backed Dr. James B. Conant's study of the American high school and his subsequent efforts. It was Carnegie that backed many of the striking innovations in North

Carolina during the governorship of Terry Sanford from 1961 to 1965, efforts that at their inception could not have been approved by the state legislature.

But the Carnegie Corporation is only one of hundreds of private foundations that have spurred the educational drive. None of them compare, of course, to the Ford Foundation, which has contributed hundreds of millions to such diverse projects as educational television, school-building studies, Negro colleges, and international education. Its "challenge grants," already made to some four dozen of the nation's best colleges and universities, form the greatest single dose of financial help in the history of private giving to education.

Not even the Ford Foundation, though, can produce the funds that the Federal Government can. When the revolution in learning sprang to life, the Government was ready. In 1950 Congress created the National Science Foundation, which has been in the forefront of planning and funding many of the experimental projects, including much of ESI's work.

The Federal Government took another significant step with the passage of the National Defense Education Act (NDEA) in 1958, which provided funds for new facilities in science, mathematics, and foreign languages. Because it came a few months after Sputnik, the NDEA is sometimes considered a reaction to that shock. But in fact, scholars had been putting together the structure of NDEA for two years; what Sputnik did was cause enough public furor to get the bill passed quickly.

All this—a greater public awareness of the problems and possibilities of education, a significant involvement by the nation's best minds, more money from both private and public sources—has combined to raise American education from a mundane to an energetic and creative level. There is no mistaking the fact that the revolution in learning has not permeated the nation's school systems; such results will take years, even decades. There is no mistaking the fact that many changes are still unproven; errors will be made and adjustments will be necessary. There is no mistaking the fact that much remains to be done—including ideas that no one has yet thought about.

There is no mistaking the fact, however, that American education has never before been so alive.

JOHN CULKIN, S.J.

Education in a Post-Literate World

Education, a seven-year-old assures me, is "how kids learn stuff." Few definitions are as satisfying. It includes all that is essential—a who, a what, and a process. It excludes all the people, places, and things which are only sometimes involved in education. The economy and accuracy of the definition, however, are more useful in locating the problem than in solving it. We know little enough about *kids*, less about *learning*, and considerably more than we would like to know about *stuff*. Marshall McLuhan has a few theories about how the world turns in 1966. Let's try him out consecutively on *kids*, *learn*, and *stuff*, realizing, as he would caution, that the three elements are intertwined in reality and that analysis in this fragmented fashion is valid only if it respects and reestablishes this unity.

Kids

Kids are what the game is all about: Given an honest game with enough equipment to go around, it is the mental, emotional, and volitional capacity of the kid which most determines the final score. The whole complicated system of formal education is in business to get through to kids, to motivate kids, to help kids learn stuff. The nature of the kids will determine the nature of the learning.

And what are 1966 American kids like? McLuhan would say that they're not very much like 1906 kids. A lot of things have happened since the turn of the century and most of them plug into walls. Today's six-year-old has already learned a lot of stuff by the time he shows up for the first day of school. Soon after his umbilical cord was cut he was planted in front of a TV set "to keep him quiet." He liked it enough there to stay for some 3,000 to 4,000 hours before school starts. He lives in a world which bombards him from all sides with information from radios, films, telephones, magazines, recordings, and people. He learns

John Culkin, S.J., "Education in a Post-Literate World," *Media and Methods*, 3, no. 3 (November, 1966), 6–9.
Father Culkin is Director of Communications at Fordham University.

more things from the windows of cars, trains, and even planes. Through travel and communications he has experienced the war in Vietnam, the wide world of sports, the civil rights movement, the death of a President, thousands of commercials, a walk in space, a thousand innocuous shows, and hopefully, plenty of Captain Kangaroo. His counterpart in 1906 lived a cloistered life by comparison.

Most of us are conscious enough of the influence of this total-information ecology on *what* kids learn. McLuhan is almost alone in stressing its impact on *how* kids learn. He claims that it is altering the psychological intake system of the kids, that it is setting up new ratios among the senses. There is no such thing as a natural sense-ratio in the sensorium, since the individual is always embedded in a culture and a language which have preferred sense-ratios. Zorba the Greek and his English boss illustrate the point nicely. Each culture develops its own sense-ratio to meet the demands of its environment. Each culture fashions its own perceptual grid and, therefore, each culture experiences reality in a unique manner. It is a question of degree. Some cultures are close enough to each other in perceptual patterns so that the differences pass unnoticed.

It is at the poles (literally and figuratively) that the violent contrasts illumine our own unarticulated perceptual prejudices. Toward the North Pole live Eskimos. The definition of an Eskimo family is a father, a mother, two children, and an anthropologist. When the anthropologist goes into the igloo he learns a lot about himself. Eskimos see pictures and maps equally well from all angles. They can draw equally well on top of a table or underneath it. They have phenomenal memories. They travel marvelously well in their white-on-white world. They have forty or fifty words for the thing we call "snow." They live in a world without linearity, a world of acoustic space. They are Eskimos. If we were to educate the two children in our kind of school, it would help to realize that they are plugged into reality on a different frequency than we are. McLuhan is suggesting that the 1966 model of the American kid is operating on a frequency just as different. The new media have made the difference. Getting through to him requires some insight into the difference.

Learn

Learning is something that people do for themselves. People, places, and things can facilitate or impede learning; they can't make it happen without some cooperation from the learner. The learner these days comes to school with a vast reservoir of vicarious experiences and loosely related facts; he is accustomed to communication through image and sound; he wants to be involved in what he is doing; he knows inchoatively that he lives in a global village, in a spaceless age; he wants to use all his senses in his learning as an active agent in the process of discovery; he knows that all the answers aren't in. The new learner is the result of the new media, according to McLuhan. And a new learner calls for a new kind of learning.

The old kind of formal learning was essentially built around the teacher and the book. Both are good things and, before launching into an analysis of the finite qualities of the printed page, it is fitting to mention that some of my best friends are books. But in keeping with the McLuhan postulate that "the medium is the message"—that the form of the medium imposes its structure and logic on the user—a school system should be at pains to know what books do to people. Everyone is familiar enough with all the enrichment to living which is mediated through fine books to allow us to pass on to the very subtle effects upon us and our culture which McLuhan attributes to the print medium itself, independent of the content involved. Whether one uses print to say that God is dead or that God is love, the structure of the medium itself remains unchanged.

An example. While lecturing to a large audience in a modern hotel in Chicago, a distinguished professor is bitten in the leg by a cobra. The whole experience takes three seconds. He is affected through touch of the reptile, the gasp of the crowd, the swimming sights before his eyes. His memory, imagination, and emotions come into emergency action. A lot of things happen in three seconds. Two weeks later he is fully recovered and wants to write up the experience in a letter to a colleague. For purposes of analogy let's presume that human experience can be measured by liquid standards (many human experiences are in reality thus measured). Let's say that his three-second adventure equals three quarts of experience. To communicate this experience through print means that it must first be broken down into parts and then mediated, eye-dropper fashion, one-thing-at-a-time, in an abstract, linear, fragmented, sequential way. That is the essential structure of print. And once a culture uses such a medium for a few centuries, it begins to perceive the world in a one-thing-at-a-time, abstract, linear, fragmented, sequential way. And it shapes its organizations and schools according to the same premises. The form of print has become the form of thought. The medium has become the message.

For centuries now, according to McLuhan, the straight line has been the hidden metaphor of literate man. It was unconsciously but inexorably used as the measure of things. It went unnoticed, unquestioned. It was presumed as natural and universal. It is neither. Like everything else it is good for the things it is good for. To say that it is not everything is not to say that it is nothing. The electronic media have broken the monopoly of print; they have altered our sensory profiles by heightening our awareness of aural, tactile, and kinetic values. This is merely descriptive; there are no value judgments being made. Print is obviously here to stay. Post-literate does not mean illiterate; it rather describes the new social environment within which print will interact with a great variety of communications media.

The new learner, who is the product of this all-at-once electronic environment, often feels out of it in a linear, one-thing-at-a-time school environment. The total environment is now the great teacher; the student has competence models against which to measure the effectiveness of his teachers. He has access to every kind of knowledge and experience, with or without the school. Nuclear students in linear schools make for some tense times in education. Students with well-developed interests in science, the arts and humanities, or current events need assistance to suit their pace, not that of the state syllabus. The straight line theory of development and the uniformity of performance which it so frequently encouraged just don't fit many needs of the new learner. Interestingly, the one thing which most of the current educational innovations share is their break with linear or print-oriented patterns, team teaching, non-graded schools, audio-lingual language training, multi-media learning situations, seminars, student research at all levels of education, individualized learning, and the whole shift of responsibility for learning from the teacher to the student. Needless to say, these are not as widespread as they should be, nor were they brought about through any conscious attention to the premises put forward by McLuhan. Like the print-oriented and linear mentality which they now modify, these premises were plagiarized from the atmosphere. McLuhan's value is in the power he now gives us to predict and control these changes.

Stuff

There is too much stuff to learn today. McLuhan calls it an age of "information overload." To help kids learn in this age, we have to introduce them to the form, structure, gestalt, grammar, and process of the knowledge involved. We have to teach them to be their own data processors and to operate through pattern recognition. We can no longer teach them all about a subject; we can teach them what a subject is all about. The arts play a new role in education because they tune up the

entire sensorium and provide fresh modes of perception. The media themselves serve both as aids to learning and as proper objects of study in
the search for an all-media literacy.

Conclusion

These things aren't true just because Marshall McLuhan says they are.
They work. They explain problems in education that nobody else is lay-
ing a glove on. When presented clearly and with all the necessary examples and footnotes added, they have proven to be a liberating force for
hundreds of teachers who were living through the tension of this cultural
fission without realizing that the causes for the tension lay outside themselves. McLuhan's relevance for education demands the work of teams
of simultaneous translators and researchers who can both shape and
substantiate the insights which are scattered through his work. Too many
people are eager to write off McLuhan or to reduce him to the nearest
and handiest platitude which explains him to them. He deserves better
and so do the kids who learn stuff. McLuhan didn't invent electricity
or put kids in front of TV sets; he is merely trying to describe what's
happening out there so that it can be dealt with intelligently. When
someone warns you of an oncoming truck, it's frightfully impolite to
accuse him of driving the thing. McLuhan can help kids to learn stuff
better.

J. A. BATTLE

The Name of the Game Is...
High Jump

The standards related to the intellect set up in the typical educational institution of our nation, from high to low, are so low that most American students are not challenged to jump over them.

But before any unfriendly critic of American education might react with, "I've been telling you all along that the public school is too easy on those kids," let me hasten to add that while the standards for many school students' learning to think may be too low, the academic standards of the school, which are largely imposed by colleges and universities, are too high.

In 1965 alone the American public school reported 830,000 dropouts, an increase of 80,000 over the previous year. There are statistics to show that the suicide rate in both school and college is increasing each year and many educators have concluded that this is due partly to high academic and social pressures. If academic pressures are too great for a number of highly selective college students, they must be far too great for the many students of the school who are not college bound.

Academic pressures are the greatest when the tasks being performed are imposed by others and when they are felt to be unimportant by those doing them. If the students in our American school should feel that the program of the school is only a meaningless obstacle course and if teachers of the school are taught in college to be only conveyors of information that the students could read better in books or learn through audio-visual aids, then it is unlikely that students will be challenged to discover and that teachers will believe that the adventure of the mind is the most joyful and exciting adventure known to man.

But if students are encouraged to find purposes in what they learn and teachers are encouraged to be more than conveyors of information, it is likely that both students and teachers will want to become intellectual probers, experimenters and explorers. If this should come about, teachers

J. A. Battle, "The Name of the Game Is . . . High Jump," *Florida Education*, 1967.

would be true professionals who could not be replaced by the tape recorder or the teaching machine and, more important, the students could be self-directed thinkers rather than memorizers of inert facts. With the accent on the life of the intellect, neither students nor teachers would find that the educational task is a bore.

A few years ago, I talked to the educational leaders of a Florida county public school system on the subject of emphasizing a program in the public school that is oriented toward the life of the intellect. I referred to the thesis of historian Henry Steele Commager that the American public school had scored a tremendous success in educating the sons and daughters of immigrants from many diverse ethnic groups and cultures to a common American citizenship, but in the area of intellectuality that the accomplishment of the school had not been so great. I agreed with Commager's view that it is now time to begin emphasizing more the life of the intellect in the American public school.

In the discussion that followed, not a single school leader expressed the belief that the school was now placing great emphasis on the intellectual life. There did seem to be, however, a sort of consensus that America, in deciding to have education for all, had precluded the life of the intellect in its public school except for a small minority of gifted pupils. Yet there was no reason to doubt that these educational leaders sincerely wanted all their students to develop more intellectual interests.

Whenever I discuss encouraging students as thinkers with those who have the responsibility for the direction of the program of our public school, I believe I sense some feeling of frustration on their part as to how they will proceed beyond the "talk stage" in this endeavor. Actually, this should be expected since so little in the teacher preparation programs of either colleges of liberal arts or education has much concern with preparing teachers for the task of educating all American children to improve their ability to think.

Even though few American colleges and universities are preparing their graduates adequately for leadership in the democratic and intellectual life, some of them as educational leaders have been most successful in encouraging this life in the school. I have personally seen a number of examples in Florida of classes composed of just typical pupils, as far as their I.Q. was concerned, who through excellent educational leadership have "caught fire" intellectually. I observed one class studying American literature in a high school with an intellectual interest higher than usual for highly selective college classes. This class was composed mostly of the members of the football team who the principal said had not previously liked literature.

I observed another class in physics that was on a high intellectual level of learning and probably most of the members of this class, if they had been in a typical school program, would have been designated as potential dropouts.

There is valid evidence that much can be done to arouse the intellectual interests of the so-called typical American public school pupil. Yet, when I made the speech in which I related Commager's theme to the Florida county school leaders, except for not being able to make the subject matter more relevant to the learner's own life, I did not realize what was the basis of the instructional difficulty.

Later, when I was discussing with several of those who had attended the meeting the need for a greater emphasis in the school on the life of the mind, it finally dawned on me that it probably was almost an impossible task to get the great majority of pupils of the American public school to gain more interest in the intellectual life if this life is defined as those school leaders were defining it. The problem was that they were defining the intellectual life as they had learned to do so in college.

College professors usually define intelligence in abstract, conceptual and logical terms. This may make sense for the intellectually elite but it does not make sense for basing a program for the early education of all the children of all the people. In this world of rapid change the type of intelligence greatly needed is closely related to life. It can be defined as the "ability to make successful and rapid adaptation to new situations and to learn from experience." It needs to include a concern with science, technology and the problems of modern society. Fortunately, this type of intelligence is possible for the public school student to achieve. So it seems that the first step toward getting the school to more effectively stimulate an interest in the life of the mind is to redefine what is meant by the life of the mind.

While most Americans may have read somewhere that seeing, hearing, smelling, tasting and touching are psychological reactions, they have been led to believe that the realm of thought is separated from the senses. Yet, psychologists tell us that the utilization of perception—the process of organizing and interpreting the sensations received through the sense organs and the central parts of the nervous system—is the process by which most of the raw materials of thinking become available. Thus, it is in guiding the child to discover new dimensions of experience through his senses that the school is offered its best possibility for encouraging the life of the mind among all its students.

Piaget, Bruner, and some other modern scholars of note who are concerned with learning have found that children are not only capable of thinking but are capable of thinking at a higher level than most adults realize. The late great physicist, Robert Oppenheimer, said that there are small children playing on the street who are capable of solving some of his greatest problems. He said children could do this because they have modes of perception which most adults have lost years ago.

In conventional educational programs usually the non-vocational subjects are taught without much relationship to life and vocational subjects are taught in a narrow utilitarian sense unrelated to the broad experiences of life. Yet psychologists tell us that instruction that promotes the intellectual life should begin with the learners' personal life experiences. Thus the students need to first learn to cope with concrete problems in their own lives. It is then natural to proceed from these concrete experiences to abstract generalizations and from this every-day reality to bold theory. In this approach the student could in a non-forced progression go from primarily concrete and simple critical thinking to a complex pattern of thought that is concerned with an expanding awareness of alternate solutions to each problem faced and to the fundamental interrelations between different phases of life that bear on solutions to problems.

Some of our finest scholars in the traditional subject areas today are emphasizing the need to learn more than substance. They are much concerned that the concepts and methods of inquiry in their subjects also be learned. Thus they want the learner to do more than repeat what is already known. They want them to be able to solve new problems for which there are no ready answers to be memorized. Yet not enough emphasis has been put on the development of the inquirer and thinker on either the school or college level. This failure is partly the result of there being few clearly defined ways of doing the task and partly because many adults do not have much faith in the potentialities of young people as thinkers.

Our American school will have to rise much above the median intellectual level of its culture if it is to be of significant help in developing the minds of our children toward intellectual interests. The majority of adults today in America, possibly without knowing it, are being starved in a kind of vast intellectual wasteland. If this is to be offset so that our children are not to become a part of this underdeveloped world of the intellect the life of the mind must be given priority in the American educational system from the first grade through college.

In an article originally prepared for a Canadian publication, Marshall McLuhan wrote recently on how the Canadian school program itself is a basic cause of its nation's great school dropout rate. McLuhan, in making his point, probably exaggerates the severity of the situation, but his statement which follows should help us to resolve not to let it happen here:

. . . students are being processed through the old fragmented specialist chopper and they might as well be on a carrousel or merry-go-round in some entertainment park. Our youngsters at school are reacting to this, dropping out of school is one response . . . When the school fails to make sense of their environment they drop out, either physically or psychologically. The psychic dropout far outnumbers the physical dropout which is also on the increase. The psychic dropout is probably about 100%.*

The Western world today is probably in the greatest period of change in history but not many of its educational programs at any level are relating their objectives to the changing needs of this world. Our time is akin to the time of which Harold Benjamin wrote when with the sabertooth tiger extinct, children were still being subjected to a curriculum for combating the extinct tiger.

If the objectives of the American education programs at all levels concerning the life of the mind are to challenge the learners, these programs must be drastically redesigned so that they can become better related to the realities of this age. In such programs, the emphasis needs to be on understanding the known while inspiring the learners to seek the unknown, on learning "facts" within a context of utilization and learning "depth" through the broad interrelationships of the different areas of knowledge. On the latter point, McLuhan in his previously mentioned article shows the need: "in physics in the last decade big discoveries have all taken place by benefit of biology and the models of structure borrowed from other areas altogether different from physics."

If school programs cannot be made more challenging to students through placing less emphasis on academic minutiae and having more emphasis on critical and creative thought, school leaders should at least for the sake of variety lower the academic standards and change the name of the game from high jump to limbo.

I believe it was Winston Churchill who said that people die from three causes: they are worked to death, worried to death or bored to death. Being bored to death is the worst way to go and thus it should be the first requisite of the excellent teacher to be interesting and not bore his students to death. One of the best ways to gain interest is to give students an intellectual challenge. If enough teachers from kindergarten through college would do this the name of our game need be neither high jump nor limbo but education.

---

* Marshall McLuhan, "From Instruction to Discovery," *Media and Methods*, October, 1966.

LOREN EISELEY

Man, Time, and Prophecy

"Former men," observed Emerson in the dramatic days of the new geological science, "believed in magic, by which temples, cities, and men were swallowed up, and all trace of them gone. We are coming on the secret of a magic which sweeps out of men's minds all vestige of theism and beliefs which they and their fathers held. . . . Nature," he contended clairvoyantly, "is a mutable cloud." Within that cloud is man. He constitutes in truth one of Emerson's most profound questions. Examined closely, he is more than a single puzzle. He is an indecipherable palimpsest, a walking document initialed and obscured by the scrawled testimony of a hundred ages. Across his features and written into the very texture of his bones are the half-effaced signatures of what he has been, of what he is, or of what he may become.

Modern man lives increasingly in the future and neglects the present. A people who essay to do this have an insatiable demand for soothsayers and oracles to assure and comfort them about the insubstantial road they tread. By contrast, I am a person known very largely, if at all, as one committed to the human past—to the broken columns of lost civilizations, to what can be discovered in the depths of tombs, or dredged from ice-age gravels, or drawn from the features of equally ancient crania. Yet as I go to and fro upon my scientific errands I find that the American public is rarely troubled about these antiquarian matters. Instead, people invariably ask: what will man be like a million years from now?—frequently leaning back with complacent confidence as though they already knew the answer but felt that the rituals of our society demanded an equally ritualistic response from a specialist. Or they inquire, as a corollary, what the scientists' views may be upon the colonization of outer space. In short, the cry goes up, Prophesy! Before attempting this dubious enterprise, however, I should like to recount the anecdote of a European philosopher who, over a hundred years ago, sensed the beginnings of the modern predicament.

It seems that along a particularly wild and forbidding section of the

English coast—a place of moors, diverging and reconverging trackways, hedges, and all manner of unexpected cliffs and obstacles—two English gentlemen were out riding in the cool of the morning. As they rounded a turn in the road they saw a coach bearing down upon them at breakneck speed. The foaming, rearing horses were obviously running wild; the driver on the seat had lost the reins. As the coach thundered by, the terrified screams of the occupants could be heard.

The gentlemen halted their thoroughbred mounts and briefly exchanged glances. The same thought seemed to strike each at once. In an instant they set off at a mad gallop which quickly overtook and passed the lurching vehicle before them. On they galloped. They distanced it.

"Quick, the gate!" cried one as they raced up before a hedge. The nearest horseman leaped to the ground and flung wide the gate just as the coach pounded around the curve. As the swaying desperate driver and his equipage plunged through the opening, the man who had lifted the bar shouted to his companion: "Thirty guineas they go over the cliff!"

"Done!" cried his fellow, groping for his wallet.

The gate swung idly behind the vanished coach and the two sporting gentlemen listened minute by minute, clutching their purses. A bee droned idly in the heather and the smell of the sea came across the moor. No sound came up from below.

There is an odd resemblance in that hundred-year-old story to what we listen for today. We have just opened the gate and the purse is in our hands. The roads on that fierce coast diverge and reconverge. In some strange manner, in a single instant we are both the sporting gentlemen intent on their wager and the terrified occupants of the coach. There is no sound on all this wild upland. Something has happened or is about to happen, but what? The suspense is intolerable. We are literally enduring a future that has not yet culminated, that has, perhaps, been hovering in the air since man arose. The lunging, rocking juggernaut of our civilization has charged by. We wait by minutes, by decades, by centuries, for the crash we have engendered. The strain is in our minds and ears. The betting money never changes hands because there is no report of either safety or disaster. Perhaps the horses are still poised and falling on the great arc of the air.

We shift our feet uneasily and call to the first stranger for a word, a sanctified guess, an act of divination. As among the ancient Greeks, chresmologues, dealers in crumbling parchment and uncertain prophecy, pass among us. I am such a one. But the chresmologue's profession demands that he be alert to signs and portents in both the natural and human worlds—events or sayings that others might regard as trivial but to which the gods may have entrusted momentary meaning, pertinence, or power. Such words may be uttered by those unconscious of their significance, casually, as in a bit of overheard conversation between two men idling on a street, or in a bar at midnight. They may also be spoken upon journeys, for it is then the man in the role of the stranger must constantly confront reality and decide his pathway.

It was on such an occasion not long ago that I overheard a statement from a ragged derelict which would have been out of place in any age except, perhaps, that of the Roman twilight or our own time. It was precisely the sort of remark that a knowledgeable Greek would have examined for a god's hidden meaning and because of which a military commander, upon overhearing the words, might have postponed a crucial battle or recast his auguries.

I had come into the smoking compartment of a train at midnight, out of the tumult of a New York weekend. As I settled into a corner I noticed a man with a paper sack a few seats beyond me. He was meager of flesh and his cheeks had already taken on the molding of the skull beneath them. His threadbare clothing suggested that his remaining possessions were contained in the sack poised on his knees. His eyes were closed, his head flung back. He either drowsed from exhaustion or liquor, or both. In that city at midnight there were many like him.

By degrees the train filled and took its way into the dark. After a time the door opened and the conductor shouldered his way in, demanding tickets. I had one sleepy eye fastened on the dead-faced derelict. It is thus one hears from the gods.

"Tickets." bawled the conductor.

I suppose everyone in the car was watching for the usual thing to occur. What happened was much more terrible.

Slowly the man opened his eyes, a dead man's eyes. Equally slowly a sticklike arm reached down and fumbled in his pocket, producing a roll of bills. "Give me," he said then, and his voice held the croak of a raven in a churchyard, "give me a ticket to wherever it is."

The conductor groped, stunned, over the bills. The dead eyes closed. The trainman's hastily produced list of stations had no effect. Obviously disliking this role of Charon he selected the price to Philadelphia, thrust the remaining bills into the derelict's indifferent hand and departed. I looked around. People had returned to their papers, or were they only feigning?

In a single sentence that cadaverous individual had epitomized modern time as opposed to Christian time and in the same breath had pronounced the destination of the modern world. One of the most articulate philosophers of the twentieth century, Henri Bergson, has dwelt upon life's indeterminacy, the fact that it seizes upon the immobile, animates, organizes, and hurls it forward into time. In a single poignant expression this shabby creature on a midnight express train had personalized the terror of an open-ended universe. I know that all the way to Philadelphia I fumbled over my seat check and restudied it doubtfully. It no longer seemed to mean what it indicated. As I left the train I passed the bearer of the message. He slept on, the small brown sack held tightly in his lap. Somewhere down the line the scene would be endlessly repeated. Was he waiting for some final conductor to say "this is the place" at a dark station? Or was there money in the paper sack and had he been traveling for a hundred years in these shabby coaches as a stellar object might similarly wander for ages on the highroads of the night?

All I can assert with confidence is that I was there. I heard the destination asked for, I saw the money taken. I was professionally qualified to recognize an oracle when I heard one. It does not matter that the remark was cryptic. Good prophecy is always given in riddles, for the gods do not reveal their every secret to men. They only open a way and wait for mortal nobility or depravity to take its natural course. "A ticket to wherever it is" carries in the phrase itself the weight of a moral judgment. No civilization professes openly to be unable to declare its destination. In an age like our own, however, there comes a time when individuals in increasing numbers unconsciously seek direction and taste despair. It is then that dead men give back answers and the sense of confusion grows. Soothsayers, like flies, multiply in periods of social chaos. Moreover, let us not confuse ourselves with archaic words. In an age of science the scientist may emerge as a soothsayer.

"The children now love luxury. They have bad manners, contempt for authority. They show disrespect for their elders and love chatter in place of exercise. They no longer rise when elders enter the room. They contradict their parents, chatter before company, rattle dishes at the table, cross their legs and tyrannize over their teachers."

—SOCRATES "On the Younger Generation"
(spoken 400 B.C.)

To What Ends Do We Teach?

Educate all the children of all the people. Nurture individuality. Promote the dignity and worth of each person. Cultivate a faith in the method of shared responsibility and intelligence. Prepare persons to make wise decisions. Produce a population of innovators. These are frequently identified as objectives of education in our society. They are fundamental concerns in producing an enlightened citizenry for a democracy.

How do you interpret the purposes of education in our society? What are the proper aims of education in a democracy such as ours? You will read many provocative articles that are intended to direct your thinking toward this question of purpose. As you read, focus your attention on the relationship of the reading to the purposes of education as you perceive those purposes. The success of your study will be determined by the extent to which you are able to reexamine what you believe within the framework of added information. What you ultimately conclude regarding the purposes of education in our society will directly influence the values and practices you retain about teaching.

Make Some Decisions About These Questions

What are your idiosyncracies? Should you cultivate them?

Is educating all children an out-of-date concept?

Should the public school become involved in teaching *values*? Why? How? What?

Does the public school have a responsibility for teaching all sides of a question?

How does one learn about democracy?

How does one learn about freedom? Where does the school fit into the picture?

Should controversial issues be discussed in public schools?

JOHN W. GARDNER

The Ten Commitments

Anyone giving thought to the tasks facing science and technology may find it useful to have in mind the problems our society faces in the years immediately ahead. Thoughtful people with time on their hands can make up their own lists; for those without time, here's mine.

Let's begin with the problem of building *an enduring peace*. It is far the most critical problem facing our nation and the world. The task is not to abolish tensions among nations, which is quite impossible, but to hold those tensions within safe bounds. This requires appropriate institutional arrangements, such as the United Nations. It requires efforts to extend the rule of law in international affairs. And it requires a base of mutual understanding. It is not necessary that all nations love one another or even that they trust one another completely. But it is necessary that they understand and tolerate one another to the point that their differences can be resolved in a just, orderly, non-violent way.

I'm not going to attempt to list these problems in any order of importance, but since we began with peace, I'll list next the related problem of *the developing nations*. The combination of poverty and rising expectations that exists among half the world's population today is as volatile and threatening in its own way as the bomb. If bridges to peace are to be built among nations, the widening economic and social chasm that divides the world today is going to have to be narrowed.

Third is the problem of *population control*. Throughout the world there is a growing awareness of the gravity of unbridled population growth and the urgency of doing something about it. Today there are about 3.3 billion people in the world. By the year 2000 it is predicted that there will be 7.5 billion, most of them hungry. And, as Harrison Brown has said, "Hungry people are combustible."

The fourth problem on my list is *equal opportunity*. There isn't any-

John W. Gardner, "The Ten Commitments," Science and Humanity Supplement of the *Saturday Review*, July 1, 1967. Copyright © 1967 by the Science and Humanity Supplement of the *Saturday Review*.

John W. Gardner, a psychologist by profession, was Secretary of Health, Education, and Welfare and generally considered the most influential intellectual in President Johnson's cabinet.

51

thing Americans have cared about more deeply throughout their history. Today, racial discrimination is the chief barrier to equality of opportunity, and is unquestionably our number one domestic problem. But the racial front is not the only one on which we are struggling to provide equality of opportunity, or equal access to the benefits of American life. There are other massive barriers to individual fulfillment—poverty, illness, ignorance, physical and mental handicaps. Our goal today is breathtaking in scope, but easy to describe. We don't want *anyone* hurt or handicapped or shut out from the life of the society by circumstances that can be prevented.

The fifth problem is closely related to the fourth. We must redouble our efforts to create *an educational system that will provide the maximum individual fulfillment for each American*. In the slums of our great cities today boys and girls who could easily be brought to the full use of their powers are left stunted, inarticulate, and angry. We need an educational system that will lift them. The complexity of our society has created spectacular requirements for educated talent. We need schools that will nurture that talent, that will awaken the spark of curiosity and eagerness to learn, that will develop individuals capable of defending their individuality in a highly organized society.

Sixth, we must bring *new life to our cities*. The city is the heart and brain of an industrial society. Yet today our cities are plagued with every conceivable ill—apathy, crime, poverty, racial conflict, slum housing, polluted air and water, inferior schools and hospitals, and hopelessly snarled transportation. The flight of industry and middle-class residents to the suburbs has left the city shorn not only of needed tax revenues, but of part of its leadership. We are going to have to do more than build bridges between the inner city and its opulent periphery. We need a totally new concept of metropolitan organization.

Seventh is the problem of our *natural environment*. We can't avoid some alteration of the natural world we live in. But man, even industrial man, is a part of nature, and must find some limit to the headlong destruction and fouling of the natural environment. How much fouled air can we breathe? How much filth can we spew into our rivers and lakes? How much bleakness and ugliness can we tolerate?

Eighth is the *reshaping of government*, the age-old problem of how best to organize ourselves to accomplish our shared purposes. We have indulged ourselves far too long in the luxury of supposing that everything in this country must change and develop except our governmental structure and processes.

Until state and local governments revamp their antiquated procedures and develop the strength to carry the heavy burdens that have been thrust upon them; until Congress faces up to the requirements of reorganization; until the Executive branch carries considerably further its present efforts to streamline its departmental structure and create mutually respecting partnerships with state, local, and nongovernmental agencies; until all these steps are underway we shall continue to be hobbled in the race with change.

My ninth problem concerns *economic growth*. Since the 1930s we have made impressive gains in stabilizing and managing the economy. Because of what we now know about the sources of economic growth we can envisage the elimination of poverty, the rebuilding of our cities, wise use of our natural resources, and more imaginative use of human skills. To the extent that we sustain a high rate of economic growth, all our other problems will be easier.

The final item on my agenda is the *relationship of the individual to society*. Everything that we do, all that we achieve, must finally be measured in terms of its effect on the individual. We set out to create a society in which the individual could flourish. But our highly organized society carries its own threats to individuality.

We can avert that threat. We can't escape size and complexity today, but we can design our institutions so that they serve the individual as well as the system. Our goal should be a society designed for people; and if we want it badly enough, we can have it.

One striking feature of our situation today is that we are creating new problems as we go along. Some of the most interesting of the new problems stem from scientific and technical advances. Consider the problems posed by some of the new mind-affecting drugs. Consider the economic, ethical, and social problems posed by the possibility of artificial organs, or weather control, or the control of genetic processes.

Our capacity to create new problems as rapidly as we solve the old has implications for the kind of society we shall have to design. We shall need a society that is sufficiently honest and open-minded to recognize its problems, sufficiently creative to conceive new solutions, and sufficiently purposeful to put those solutions into effect. It should be, in short, a self-renewing society, ready to improvise solutions to problems it won't recognize until tomorrow. The vitality of our science and technology will have a good deal to do with whether we achieve that kind of society.

GEORGE B. LEONARD

The Real Crisis in Education

The most explosive subject in this country is no longer religion or politics. It is schools. Education became public issue number one around the time of the first Sputnik in 1957. Since then, the feelings of millions of parents have gone from concern to obsession to near hysteria.

Those most vehement in the Great Education Debate usually have assumed that the major purpose of the public schools is to prepare students for college, that the purpose of college is to prepare them for personal success, and that perhaps the ultimate purpose of the whole process is to make our nation stronger than its potential enemies.

In all the talk about school, vocational education until now has rarely been mentioned. All has changed. After years of neglect, vocational-technical training has become a hot issue. This spring, in fact, it is being pushed as a solution for every problem from high-school dropouts to juvenile delinquency and unemployment. Recent magazine articles have followed this panacea tack. In Washington, President Kennedy gave top priority to improved job training in our schools. Republican strategists are supporting more vocational education as an *alternative* to Democratic-sponsored youth-employment bills. The President wanted both.

Much of the credit for the new, urgent national interest in school job training must go to the President's Panel of Consultants on Vocational Education. This group, headed by Chicago school superintendent Benjamin Willis, released its final report in April. The report details the chilling employment statistics presented on preceding pages of this story and sets forth strengths and weaknesses in American schooling for "the world of work." It ends with a recommendation that Federal spending for vocational education be increased more than fivefold, to the total of $400 million next year. Since the panel members represented opposing viewpoints, the report bears the invisible scars of compromise. It offers few if any new ideas.

Arguments on means aside, everyone agrees that some change must be

George B. Leonard, "The Real Crisis in Education," *Look*, June 4, 1963. By permission of the editors of *Look* Magazine, copyright ©, 1963, Cowles Communications, Inc.

made in the way we educate those millions who are not going to finish college. The present crisis does not signify a deterioration of our schools or a sudden jump in dropouts. Just the opposite: The percentage of young Americans graduating from high school has risen from six percent in 1900 to 17 percent in 1920 to an all-time high of 65 percent today. Then what is wrong? This: Today's complex, technological society has become entirely unforgiving of the untrained. Young people who once could have worked as unskilled factory or farm laborers have no place to go but street corners.

In coast-to-coast visits to vocational schools and interviews with leading educators, *Look* has confirmed that more and better vocational education is one of the answers to the problems of the noncollege graduate. But it is not the only answer. And it holds dangers that are not being aired in the current public statements on the subject.

Start with Connecticut, which boasts the best statewide system of vocational schools in the nation. Its 14 trade schools are operated by the state, rather than by local school districts. Students may travel beyond their own districts to get the vocational and technical training they wish— but only if they qualify. Right now, barely a third of those who apply are accepted by Connecticut's fine vocational schools. The state's two postgraduate technical institutes are even more exclusive. Junior-high school principals complain, only half jokingly, that "it's easier to get into Yale than into the vocational and technical schools."

Throughout the nation, vocational schools are raising their standards. This rise will improve the quality of training. And it will brighten the public "image" of vocational education—which certainly needs brightening. But it will not help the slow student who is most likely to become a dropout. Low admission standards don't seem to help him either. In those big-city vocational schools that make no attempt to keep out slow students, the dropout rate generally is higher than in academic or comprehensive high schools. "Vocational education is *not* the big answer to dropouts," Daniel Schreiber, chief of a dropout project for the National Education Association, told *Look*.

Vocational education can be quite effective as an aid in solving youth unemployment. Seymour Wolfbein, director of the Office of Manpower, Automation and Training of the U.S. Department of Labor, was emphatic on this point. "Scratch an unemployment problem," he told *Look*, "and you find a vocational-education problem. We'll need five million new skilled laborers in the next ten years. We're training about a fifth of this." Many experts shake their heads at the spectacle of skilled jobs going begging while millions of the unskilled can find no work.

But even as an antidote to joblessness, vocational education has limits.

Today, the most effective trade schools, in close cooperation with labor and industry, train students for specific jobs (plasterer, sheet-metal worker, machinist, etc.). But in this swift-changing world, specific skills constantly move toward obsolescence, while new, strange skills suddenly pop out of nowhere. Said Wolfbein, "Even if the schools were doing good vocational education, we'd have to have postgraduate retraining in the future. Look at the ads for technicians in the New York *Times*. There are words there not even *existing* five years ago."

Students Despise Academics

A growing number of schools offer vocational training after high school. High schools that attempt to give both full-scale vocational training *and* the regular high-school curriculum often succeed at neither. These schools are dreary places. Three hours a day of shop leave time for only a skeletal academic program. What happens? Academic subjects tend to be taught in a dry, perfunctory way that serves to reinforce the dislike for bookwork many students bring with them from home and earlier schooling. Almost every vocational student interviewed by *Look* said he despised academics. "What I like about this school," a Georgia electronics student emphasized, "is that you don't have to take social science and literature and art. That stuff is good for conversation and social affairs, but there's no other use for it."

Here is deep irony: The U.S. work-week, already short, is almost certain to become even shorter in the future. Skilled craftsmen, now training in vocational schools, will have more leisure time than any other job group. But it is they who are getting the least experience in activities that will make leisure creative rather than destructive. The age of automation holds few threats more ominous than an overdose of free time for those unprepared to use it.

The worst thing about all-out vocational training at the high-school level is that it forces the student to choose his trade, his slot in the work force, at the age of 13 or so. Good vocational schools try to keep the way clear for students to change vocations throughout their school careers. But the average student finds it difficult, if not impossible, to make a change after the tenth grade.

If vocational training as it now exists should be crammed into more and more high schools, it could well change the entire structure of our society. As in Europe (where the educational system is now undergoing reform), a majority of our young people would have their lives decided for them just when they enter their teens. They might develop into efficient human tools in the technological machine. But they would have no opportunity to develop to the full as human beings.

The history of vocational education in America has been a sequence of crisis actions. This type of schooling has flourished in wars and national emergencies. Today, we are cheating millions of students by failing to give them job training. But we would also be cheating them with new crash programs that treat human beings as means, not ends. Some situations—notably in the centers of the big cities and in depressed areas—cry out for specific job training at the high-school level. But far better are programs that retain the richness and diversity of the best secondary schools, reserving the years *after* high school for specific job training. Such is the opinion of many educators interviewed by *Look*.

What may be needed is an entirely new way of handling the non-academic student in high school. One plan would create a high-school "technical track" that would enroll practical-minded students who are not necessarily planning to finish a four-year college course. This track would teach the basics of our technological age—mathematics, practical physics, blueprint reading and the like—and would replace the conventional three-hour-a-day shop period with one-hour "tech lab," relating closely to the basic subjects. That would still leave time for the other elements of the American high-school experience: humanities, citizenship training, art, music and—also important—extracurricular activities.

Technical-track graduates would go on to specific job training in concentrated post-high-school programs. Or they would attend technical institutes to become technicians or engineering aides. They could even go on to a four-year college—or leave the vocational-technical field entirely.

An experimental technical-track program is under way in two Richmond, Calif., high schools and may expand to seven more California schools. Reports Marvin Feldman, director of the program, "Though it's still experimental, it looks so good we're holding our breath."

We've Got to Catch Them Early

Many educators interviewed by *Look* insisted that vocational training not be treated in a vacuum apart from the rest of the educational process. The solution for the dropout problem, they argue, starts not in trade school, but in the first grade.

A child's earliest lesson is simply this: He discovers that learning is exciting, challenging, a pleasure. Or he finds it a sort of meaningless hell that he will try to avoid as long as he lives. To make learning a pleasure requires knowledge, skill and direction of a high order, especially in working with children who come from culturally deprived homes. The best teachers may be the true heroes and saints of this age.

Some educators fear that the present school atmosphere of pressure and near hysteria is the worst possible environment for making learning a pleasure. Part of the blame for this must go to those critics of American education who rode high in the years following Sputnik. At best, they demanded better teacher education, an end to extremes of permissiveness and an emphasis on the basic subjects. At worst, they engaged in meaningless diatribes about terminology ("progressive," "life adjustment," etc.) and made vague and threatening demands for "excellence" and "rigor"—which they rarely if ever defined in operational terms. Most incredible of all was their claim that it matters not in the least "how to teach" if the teacher knows "what to teach." ("Anyone who says that should have his head examined," educator and philosopher Harold Taylor told *Look*. "Or, better yet, he should be sentenced to attend a week of lectures by a subject-matter specialist who doesn't know how to communicate with students.")

Teachers and school administrators were badly frightened by the critics' attacks. What could they do? In all the semantic nonsense assaulting them, the teachers found one prescription that lent itself to action: "Get tough!" Many, many teachers did just that. Often without improving the quality of the material or the presentation, they doubled their demands on students. It is doubtful that the students are learning more than they would with *half* the work intelligently and imaginatively assigned. What they are mainly learning is to despise school and all intellectual activity.

This state of affairs, writes Professor Nevitt Sanford, director of the Institute for the Study of Human Problems at Stanford University, can create a "slave mentality" in students. "We are not proceeding in a way that will give us excellence in performance on the job or in life. Our student-slaves might be suitable technicians in the future, but it is a little hard to imagine their becoming leaders of society . . . or well-developed individuals."

Again, we are face to face with the assumption that human beings—be they in vocational school, academic school, grade school or college—can be treated as means rather than as ends in themselves.

Instead of "getting tough" and making the learning process as unpleasant as possible, educators would do better to join in the search for improved methods of teaching and learning that will make our schools more effective, more pleasant and more *human*. Significantly, most critics of modern American education are not to be found in the forefront of those calling for new and better methods of teaching. Among *their* more imaginative ideas is the proposal that we go back to *McGuffey's Reader*.

Despite their longing for a dear, dead world, the last few years have seen the development of several promising new learning methods. For example, recent experiments in programmed instruction (*Look*, June 5, 1962) suggest that every child, except the seriously retarded, can learn to read—*with pleasure*. And lack of reading ability is at the very heart of the dropout problem.

Another factor in the destructive pressure brought to bear on today's students is the rat race for college degrees. "Today, attendance at college . . . ," John W. Gardner, president of the Carnegie Corporation of New York, has observed, "becomes, in the false value framework we have created, the only passport to happiness."

The greatest danger in education today—whether vocational or college —is that human beings will be treated as nothing more than slaves of schools and tools of society. John Gardner and others have pointed out that education in the future will not end with any certificate of graduation; people will go "back to school" perhaps several times in their lives.

This itself will help destroy the artificial emphasis on certain types of education. "Emphasis will be on individual fulfillment and personal growth, however they may best be furthered," writes Gardner, "and they will be sought for all."

"*If a nation expects to be ignorant and free . . . it expects what never was and never will be.*"

—THOMAS JEFFERSON

HAROLD TAYLOR

Students, Teachers, Values

In preparation for my lecture this afternoon, I turned up an unlikely looking bundle of mimeographed sheets which only my habits of thrift had preserved and I found there some valuable remarks by the late President Lowell, of Harvard University, about earthworms. The earthworms were under study at Harvard. It was early in this century, at a time when psychology was just beginning to assert its claim to know something about learning, and psychologists were becoming interested in education. This meant that college presidents were becoming interested in psychologists.

Accordingly, Mr. Lowell visited Professor Yerkes' laboratory one day to see what was afoot. It was mostly animal psychology in those days, apes, dogs, cats, brass instruments. Mr. Lowell found Professor Yerkes experimenting with earthworms; they were spending their psychological time crawling down a maze and at a given point in the maze, where the route was blocked, approximately half of them went to the left, and the other half turned right.

The earthworms who turned right were given the standard psychologists' treatment of that time, an electric shock. After that, 75 per cent of them turned left on the next run. The other anti-intellectuals, the 25 per cent of them, kept right on going right.

After noting these results Mr. Lowell made what seems to me to be one of the most profound remarks in the history of American education. He said, "They have been changed by this Harvard course, but I can't say they are any better earthworms for having been at Harvard."

I hope very much that the story is true, since Mr. Lowell's remark burrows beneath the surface of educational clichés and turns up a large mound of interesting questions. It raises the question of values.

For example, it suggests that the first thing to decide about education is the question of what changes education can actually make in human nature? How much of education is conditioned reflex? Social conditioning? Mental conditioning?

It raised the question of what changes in human nature are most

Harold Taylor, *Students, Teachers, Values*, Spaulding Lecture, Yale University, April 19, 1960.

desirable? Then we must ask, how do you go about deciding whether a change is for the better or the worse? Or we might ask, if it is possible for education to change human nature, isn't it dangerous to turn teachers loose with the personality of a child? Should the educators be allowed to make whatever changes they please? How do they know they are succeeding, if they are? Or if teachers should not decide on the changes to be made, who should? Parents? Clergymen? School Boards? Politicians? The American Legion? The Federal Government? Or if you believe that human nature can and should be changed, what do you say to those who believe that the whole matter is settled by Freud or by God before the child ever gets to school?

Education, a Process of Growth and Development

The important fact is that this way of looking at education turns our attention away from education as such and toward human nature and human beings. Education is usually considered to be the acquisition of knowledge, the taking of subjects and courses, when in fact it is nothing of the kind. It is a process of growth and development which takes place in students when they work at it under favorable or unfavorable circumstances. The content of education is not a body of knowledge. It is a cluster of attitudes, feelings, perceptions, insights, abilities and skills, of which the ability to think independently and clearly is of the first importance, and the ability to experience life fully and honestly is certainly no less valuable.

Knowledge, as far as education is concerned, is a means to this end and not an end in itself. For the student, there is no knowledge until the student involves himself in getting it, it is not so much knowledge as knowledge-getting. Otherwise a body of knowledge is simply a name for organized information, and until the student does something with it, it is only a set of materials waiting to be transformed into living thoughts, ideas and attitudes.

In other words, knowledge exists as something known by someone, it has no independent reality of its own, it merely seems to be real because it can be written out in words, symbols and numbers. This is also the reason why so few educators realize that paintings, sculpture, dance and music are forms of knowledge, even though they do not express themselves in words. They can of course be talked about and written about, but that is the least important thing about them. The important thing is the experience of them for the participant in the arts, the experience of forms of reality which are different from those which can be expressed in words.

The student is educated by the experiences he undergoes and the quality of his education depends on the depth and quality of those experiences. His attitudes, including his attitude to education and to learning are affected by the people he admires, the experiences he enjoys, the expectations others have of him.

In this the student is no different from the rest of the human race, and, as a matter of fact, the experience of the student outside the academic program and outside the school and college itself is often as important or more important in terms of educational and intellectual influence than anything he may learn in the regular curriculum. As William James used to say, the history of philosophy is the history of the temperaments of philosophers. Individuals become devoted to certain ideas and values because they prefer them to others, because of the congenial relationships which exist between individuals and the ideas in which they believe.

It works the other way around, too, fortunately, that is to say, certain ideas are persuasive in and of themselves, and once recognized as valuable and interesting, do change the intellectual temperament of those affected by them. The danger is that fashions develop among ideas, and it is often difficult for young people to resist the persuasion of fashion and the social pressure of intellectual prestige.

A whole generation of students of literature tried their best to gain a tragic and doomed attitude to life because of the influence of T. S. Eliot, and it is hard to say whether or not the late Forties was a genuinely anxious time for the young or whether young critics and writers were merely doing their best to give content to Mr. Auden's term, The Age of Anxiety.

Immediate Impact of Their Society Important to Students

This is why it is of such very great importance to bring to each generation of students the immediate impact of their society and the original materials of social, scientific and philosophic thought, to make every effort to allow them to approach it freshly, without prior instructions as to the categories and trends into which the material should fit. They must be asked to read the work of Descartes, or Swift or Dylan Thomas for themselves, without commentary, guides and instructions, so they may establish a direct relationship between the author's ideas and their own.

Otherwise the student picks up phrases about Descartes' dualism, Swift's loathing of humanity, or Thomas' lyricism which are useful as tags but which usually block the student's perception of the ideas of the author and, in a sense, do all the work for the students by giving him reputable classifications for ideas which he has not made part of his own knowledge.

The student must be allowed to make his own effort to understand, otherwise he will take the easy way of following established opinion, which although it may possibly be sound, is not educationally valuable to the person who substitutes it for his own.

In order not to be swept along in intellectually fashionable currents, the student must learn how to establish his own identity, an intellectual and personal identity which is his and no one else's. This is a question not of teaching the student what to believe, but of teaching him how to find out what he believes, about himself and his world, about other people and ideas, to find ways of knowing who he is, what are his talents, what are his strengths, what are his weaknesses, to learn what there is in life, what he wants from life, and what he can give to life. All this is involved in the conduct of education.

Values Being Taught All the Time

What I am trying to say is that education in schools and colleges, as distinct from education outside these institutions, consists of students and teachers and their values. It is nonsense to ask, Does education have anything to do with values? or, Can values be taught?

Values are being taught all the time, both in and out of educational institutions, although it is, in my judgment, of very great importance that educational institutions consciously take account of the fact that their purpose is to give to their students an awareness of standards and values and that even when they say it isn't and act as if it weren't they are teaching a certain kind of value, in this instance a kind of negativism.

The teacher who gives grudgingly of time taken away from his research and thinks of his teaching as an obligation rather than a delight. is teaching students something about themselves—in this instance that they are not worth bothering with. They then ask, Why bother?

Responsibility of School and College

The life of a student is saturated with values of all kinds, and it is the responsibility of the school and college to provide a variety of experience for the student from which he may learn to value certain forms of experience as of greater importance than others. If the variety of experience is limited to classroom academic study and the social life of clubs, fraternities and sports, he is likely to remain untouched by any of the true values of higher learning. Again, it is a matter of his coming alive as a person.

Martha Graham put it directly in her own way, in a conversation one day in a taxi-cab with Agnes de Mille. Miss Graham said, "There is a vitality, a life-force, an energy, a quickening which is translated through you into action, and because there is only one of you in all time, this expression is unique. And if you block it, it will never exist through any other medium and be lost. The world will not have it."

Liberal education, as I would define it, is the means by which the student achieves his selfhood. To achieve the flavor of individuality one does not try to be an individual. Individualism is achieved by trying to be honest with oneself in one's own judgments and preferences, and individualism is an outcome of that effort, not its purpose.

It is necessary to give up wanting to be liked, wanting to have everything smooth and easy, otherwise what we get in the individual is a cluster of approved characteristics. It is necessary to discover this by oneself.

No one can make these discoveries except by individual effort, and life in the college of liberal arts must be organized in such a way that the student is continually thrust into situations from which he must extricate himself by his own efforts, with such help as may be useful to that end.

The trouble is that most kinds of education are devoted to teaching students not how to be themselves, but instead how to cover up, how to gain enough knowledge, for example, in a survey course in Western literature that no one will ever know you haven't read any of the authors or even understood what they really meant.

The usual kind of education, the kind that is divided up into courses, condensed into textbooks, put in three lectures a week, tested by examinations, and rewarded by three academic credits a throw is designed to give answers to questions nobody asked and to prevent the student from ever having to admit his own ignorance. It is a way in which he can cover up his true self by finding a vocabulary acceptable to most people and a set of facts generally known among people considered to be educated.

By this approach you may never be called upon to say what you really think or feel at any point in your education. This is what makes bores, and produces college graduates who are ignorant and dull but successful and plausible. For a teacher who cares about teaching, there is nothing as exciting as students who are ignorant, who come to you uncorrupted by knowledge of the things you know most about.

I think it is wrong to judge students, especially when they are freshmen, only by how much they know, since if they know everything they should, there would be no need for them to be in college. That is what was wrong with Mr. Hutchins' College at the University of Chicago. It had a peculiar conception of the intellect. In order to get in you passed examinations in all the things they had to teach there, so the best student was the one who passed all the tests for admission at the age of thirteen or so and didn't have to go there at all.

What Martha Graham has said, not only in the remark I read to you just now, but through her total attitude to life and the expression of her art, defines an idea which should infuse any philosophy of education designed to release the talents of individuals. The forms of the dance which Martha Graham has created are free forms, that is to say, they are forms newly created to express new truths which she found impossible to express in any of the ways dancers, choreographers and playwrights had taken before her. There was an energy in American life which she felt, the same force which Whitman recognized and which he too created new forms to express.

But the way to find that form of energy which is truly our own—not European, not Russian, not anything but itself—is to learn how to be sincere and honest in one's feelings and taste, how to be bold and courageous enough freely to like something, to recognize something which perhaps no one else will either like or approve, but nevertheless to recognize it, work with it, try it out, fearing neither success nor failure, courting no approval and posing no martyrdom, but doing everything in one's power to look at things freshly and honestly. This to me is the way to personal independence and personal freedom, a quality which it will be clear by now I value as a primary aim for the student in his education.

What Is a Value?

What, then, is a value, and how is it reached through education?

Stripped of its technical definition, a value is clearly a name for something which people value. It indicates an act of choice, a preference, a judgment on the part of one who makes a choice. People value freedom because of the richness it can bring to their lives, and freedom is therefore said to be a value. If it brings no richness, or if people do not wish to use it, they do not value it, although it may still remain as a value for others. Freedom is an idea on which people act, as in South Africa or Alabama, or it may be said to be a principle which is invoked as a reason for action.

Instead of asking, What are values? as if values were forms or things in a separate realm of abstraction, we should ask, What do people value? On what grounds do they make their choices? Then the active, immediate and personal quality comes out, and it is clear that the abstractions—justice, freedom, equality, integrity—are only abstractions until the individual human being acts in such a way it can be seen that he values in reality the forms of conduct which they represent.

If education has to do with values, these abstractions must be reduced to something more specific before they can be dealt with. To state it another way, education is the instrument by which students learn to prefer one thing to another and to acquire a set of ideas in which they believe and on which they can act.

Educators Should Know Quite a Lot About Their Students

As educators we are concerned to deepen the response of the student to certain facts and experiences in human life which artists, scholars, poets, painters, sculptors, architects, writers, scientists, philosophers, and others have found to be of a richer and more important kind than those which the student has as yet had the opportunity to discover. Some of them he may, of course, have already discovered, and in forming a curriculum, it is important not to repeat for him a lesson in discovery which is no longer needed. This means that educators should know quite a lot about their students before they decide what should be taught that is not already known.

There is a difference in quality of experience between reading an article in *Time* and listening to a Beethoven quartet. But for the student to understand the value of Beethoven or of quartets, it is not necessary for him to give up reading *Time* (although that might be a first step) nor to rate other composers and other forms of music in a kind of hierarchy of value which is certified by tradition and respectable criticism. Nor is it wise to teach Beethoven didactically, to assert Beethoven's claim to one's respect by authoritative references.

Beethoven must be allowed to win his own way into the student's consciousness and respect by allowing the student to experience Beethoven's music, carry with it the weight of critical opinion, and the authority of his place in musical history. The student cannot avoid being influenced by the reputation which accompanies the composer's work. But until he learns to enjoy the music through his own experience with it, the student has not transcended the limitations of an obligatory attitude and a sense of aesthetic duty.

For this reason, among others, it is a fallacy to assume that "Western values" are contained in the classic works of the West and that an appreciation of Western values is best induced by a presentation of the classics in a serial order to beginning students. There are certain ideas, such as the dignity of the individual, the enjoyment of life, liberty, and if possible, happiness, which are central to the forms of society we have built in the Western world.

But to value them is to do more than read about them in the classical authors and pass tests on what has been said. Quite often the student is unable honestly to value the classical authors as authors, since the style of argument or form of expression of the Great Book may be one to which he is not yet capable of adequate response.

In any case, the values in which we as educators are interested are not contained in this sense in the great works. The works are expressions of ideas, and the values they express must become part of the consciousness and emotional life of the student before they have an effect on his attitudes and actions.

The Climate of the College

The value of liberty and justice is likely to affect the student more deeply by the action of his university in opposing a loyalty oath, upholding a faculty member's right of free speech against a Congressional Committee, or insisting on unsegregated fraternities than by his reading of philosophical texts.

The way the teacher presents the classical authors, the characteristics of the educational system in which the student is taught may have more effect on his attitudes toward the ideas of the authors than anything contained in the works themselves. The climate of the college may, in many cases, be anti-intellectual and emotionally luke-warm, so what is learned is a mechanical method for dealing with literary and philosophical materials as part of a general effort to "get through" college and move on as quickly as possible to more important things which are really valued such as making money and being successful.

In fact, this is what more commonly happens. Our studies of students' values show very little relation between the materials of the curriculum and the attitudes of students. According to one large segment of contemporary research, the greatest influence on the value-system of college students comes from the attitudes of other students and the social patterns of the community outside the college and high school. The trouble is that too often the life of the campus reflects the values of its surrounding society when it should be creating new values for a changing society.

Student Aims

I have with me a statement from a college student in an institution which I shall not name other than to say that it is in New Jersey, in a moderate-sized town called Princeton. The statement is one made on behalf of his generation. The young man had been asked by a member of the faculty to state what his values were, to which he replied, in part:

"Success for me would mean a job that I could leave after eight hours and that would provide self-fulfillment within a framework of inconspicuous luxury."

Said another student who did not share this modest aim but demanded something more, "We've replaced the ideal of splendid excellence with a new ideal of competent decency." The ideal had become flattened out in the course of contemporary history, until right from the kindergarten to the college, the student wished to be adjusted, well-liked, popular, noticed and successful. The aim was to be well-rounded, well-rounded, that is, in the sense that all the rough edges had been rubbed off until a man was perfectly round like a tennis ball, with a little friendly fuzz on top. "It is quite another to want the calm itself, without the storm."

The process by which the younger generation has achieved its present system of values of course complex, and it is not my purpose here today to add to the literature of criticism of youth, particularly since youth has demonstrated a capacity for self-criticism which caused another of its members to refer to it as the "generation of the third eye, the eye of self-consciousness."

It is my view that this generation has been taught to be self-conscious, analytical, guarded and reserved by its teachers, its parents and its society. The generation has responded to the attitude and expectations of an older generation which has demanded little of itself and has expected little from the world. To act spontaneously, earnestly or enthusiastically in personal social issues has been considered gauche and a sign of immaturity.

In discussions of education recently I have been told many times that students are not ready or able to make up their minds on questions of importance, since they do not know enough; they first need to be told, and the task of the teacher is to give instruction to those who need to be told, not to answer student questions or to expect students to answer their own.

I have been told, too, that most contemporary issues are too complicated for anyone to solve and that only a fool would try to give answers to questions which puzzle even the most informed and experienced of experts.

The effect of such views on my own educational ideas has been negligible, but when they are presented often enough to students by teachers who sincerely hold them, the effect is to persuade students that a guarded silence and more study is the only sensible course for a serious person to follow.

I have also noticed that as the ability of students to handle academic materials has increased under more highly selective admissions requirements, university teachers have increased their emphasis on the purely academic side of the student's education. The curriculum reforms which college faculties have made are aimed, as one student put it, "at exploiting this greater scholastic potential."

This has put a premium on two things, the student's ability to cover a larger and larger body of material, and his ability to think, speak and write in the accepted pattern of academic discourse. Not only is there no impetus given to the student's need to think for himself, but even if he wants to, there is no time for him to do it. He is kept too busy covering the acres of academic material to have a chance to think, even about the material he is covering.

True Ends of Education

Added to this is a heavy emphasis on competitive success in achieving high grades, both for admission to graduate school and for building a record which can attract the best potential employers. When we remember that the pressure for academic grades now begins in the freshman and sophomore year in high school, increases as the fearful time of college admission comes on, and continues through every year of college, it is clear that the whole thing has gotten out of hand, and that we have lost sight of the true ends of education by confusing them with a set of mechanical academic means.

These are the ways the teaching programs of the educational institutions are affecting the values of students when they have any effect at all. They are having the negative or a quiescent effect. Occasionally something a little gayer happens when the effect is to cause students to reject the value system of the university and strike out for themselves. The central educational element which is missing in the university as it is now organized is a relationship of mutual understanding and respect between the student and the teacher.

I have said earlier that education consists of students and teachers and their values. The teacher who is himself interested in students, devoted to the life of scholarship, passionate in his commitment to intellectual affairs and concerned that his students learn to understand and to love the life of the mind will find that his students learn to love many of the things which he loves, and that they share his attitude to learning itself.

A System with Central Concern for the Student

But it is necessary for the institution itself to devise a system in which the student is the central concern, since the student is the reason for the existence of a university. Otherwise the university becomes either a research center or a library, two kinds of institutions which are adjuncts to a university but not its reason for existence.

Kierkegaard has defined the teacher who understands the university in this sense. He says, ". . . if you can find exactly the place where the other is and begin there, you may perhaps have the luck to lead him to the place where you are.

"For to be a teacher does not mean simply to affirm that such and such a thing is so, or to deliver a lecture, etc. No, to be a teacher in the right sense is to be a learner. Instruction begins when you, the teacher, learn from the learner, put yourself in his place so that you may understand what he understands and in the way he understands it, in case you have not understood it before. Or if you have understood it before, you allow him to subject you to an examination so that he may be sure you know your part. This is the introduction. Then the beginning can be made in another sense."

Because we wish to make this new kind of beginning, some of us reject all standard programs of required studies, all the mechanical apparatus of the academic credit system, all the destructive intellectual habits of grade-getting and competition for marks, all the boredom and futility of the lecture system and return to simpler ways of life and learning, in an effort to make education natural, joyful, intuitive, and useful, to return to the original sources of human knowledge in personal discovery, exchange of ideas, in intellectual curiosity, in imagination, in the creative arts, in the practice of science and scientific thinking, in the immediate experience of social reality.

The Place to Begin

We wish to remove the inhibitions of the textbooks, the anthologies, the survey courses. We wish to have the student come close to the origins of his culture, to work in materials which are chosen not with a view to forcing him to do an intellectual duty but with a view to engaging him in an enterprise of intellectual and personal excitement.

Do not prescribe all subjects, begin at the place where the student is to take him from there to the next place. I wish to have us extend to the whole of education an idea which is central to Ortega in the conduct of his thought. "There is but one way to save a classic," said Ortega, "to give up revering him and use him for our own salvation—that is to lay aside his classicism, to bring him close to us, to make him contemporary, to set his pulse going again with an injection of blood from our veins, whose ingredients are our passions . . . and our problems."

When we do this, we affect the values of our students. We build a community of students and teachers in which ideas become urgent and actions become infused with thought and imagination. In this way we help the student to form a philosophy whose principles continue to be tested and re-created in a personal way through the rest of his life.

Cold War Fallout in the Public Schools

Those of us employed in public schools have become aware of a tightening up process that began in earnest almost four years ago when the Soviet Union's space satellite dramatically alerted the nation to its educational shortcomings. Since that time school officials and parents alike have increasingly and more energetically concerned themselves with the staggering task of overhauling mediocre curricula and improving teaching methods, as well as with the search for talented teachers at all levels of the educational structure.

In this sense the intensity of heat generated by the Cold War with Russia has already had salutary effects on the American educational scene. But not all of the "fallout" that has filtered into the classroom has been so positive. The American school faces not only the threat posed by the Soviet Union and the fact that the communists have been pouring three times as much money into education in relation to gross national product, as the United States. A more subtle threat is posed by the effects of cold war competition. This is the tendency to compromise traditional ideologies that have characterized American education in the past under the pressure of national anxiety and the resulting desire to do anything which will help us keep pace with the Russians and prove to ourselves our educational adequacy.

Proof of the Pudding

The parents of our pupils, understandably influenced by the rash of alarmist school criticism, have been more vocal than even in demanding tangible proof of the education pudding. How many times has a beleaguered school superintendent or principal stood up before a jury of parents at a PTA meeting and sought, with the aid of glossy graphs,

Paul P. Mok, "Cold War Fallout in the Public Schools," *The Harvard Graduate School of Education Bulletin*, Fall, 1961.

charts, filmstrips and other audio-visual paraphernalia, to present the defense of his implicitly indicted school!

"Look at our pupils' test scores," he rails, "our sixth graders last year scored almost a year and a half above the national norms on a standardized examination in language usage! Look at the artist's sketch for the proposed new junior high school! Look at the new closed-circuit educational television schedule! Look, look, look!"

He sounds like the pitchman of old, but he is not selling a bottle of tonic guaranteed to cure backache, rheumatism, tired blood, and middle-age depression—instead he is trying, as never before in his life, to seel his

He sounds like the pitchman of old, but he is not selling a bottle of age depression—instead he is trying, as never before in his life, to sell his school and its program to a critical public. The pressure we feel upon us to sell our programs, our services, our very selves as professional educators, demands a great toll on our energies and time and imagination—and even the rank and file classroom teacher has become an apprentice pitchman in the process.

A school system perpetually on the defensive is a school system that feels guitly. In order to expiate that guilt, be it rationally or irrationally determined, we are in danger of investing greater energy toward seeking approval than in addressing ourselves to tasks which may not be currently fashionable and therefore low in approval value.

For example, the ideology of recognizing and developing individual differences represents a traditional commitment in the American public school. Not so in the Soviet Union. There, human resources are viewed as national commodities to be developed along the lines of economic and strategic need, with individual choice playing a secondary role at best. If an individual pupil demonstrates tendencies that are not considered proper or valuable to his superiors in the educational structure, their development is not encouraged.

In the admittedly less efficient American system of public education, considerable attention has been given to the task of liberating and fortifying individual skill and talent along the lines of the pupil's naturally demonstrated interests. One is forced to wonder whether such idealism is currently being shunted into the back seat of the American education vehicle at the expense of the all powerful College Entrance Examination Board tests, the approved and fashionable extracurricular activities, and the high grade-point class standings.

Choice vs. Structure

Suppose that you, as a classroom teacher, designate a certain hour of the day as a "choice" time— a practice quite common in most elementary schools until the "fallout" of fear and anxiety become heavy in the classroom atmosphere. You feel that the time is justified because it may foster self-directed activities on the part of the youngsters. One seven-year-old boy spends the hour apparently scribbling on one sheet of paper after another until he has amassed a pile of forty-odd sheets on the floor. Each contains a mass of finely detailed but seemingly unrelated lines.

You watch the boy take his chair up to the bulletin board where he tacks up one sheet, then another, and another. The pieces fit together, each sheet a mosaic square. Spellbound, you watch as the forty-odd squares are transformed before your eyes into a mural. It is Saint George slaying the dragon. One square is the knight's gauntlet, another the hilt of his sword, another part of the blade, and so on.

You would like to get up before the throng of critical parents and defend the choice time. You know it is regarded as unnecessary, a valuable block of time in the school days which many pupils may be wasting to some degree. The parents are demanding more structured activities, an assurance that the schedule is as rigorous and demanding as possible. You would like to say that the youngster who did the mural did something in an original way—did something which you as his teacher could not have structured because you do not see things in the child's way. You would like to say that the boy's self-initiated project may have given him great satisfaction, may have excited the other children in the class, may be an important link in the development of a unique creative potential and original point of view which needs nurturing.

But many classroom teachers do not get up before the critical throng and make these statements. They recognize them as speculative. Intuitively they feel they are right, but they sense that anxious parents do not wish to hear intuitions and speculations. Instead, critics want evidence —tangible proof that what the child is doing today will help him meet society's competitive pressures, be they in the form of a 500-plus College Board score, admission into a first group college, or a class standing in the upper quartile.

If the public school has to prove—or feels it has to prove—the value of everything it is doing on the spot to a critical jury, it is going to move more and more in the direction of undertaking what can be proved readily. This is indeed unfortunate and frightening. Will the classroom teacher devote as much time to those activities which may not bear tangible results until the pupil is many years older? One teacher of my acquaintance, for example, used to allow her pupils approximately thirty minutes per day to write several paragraphs of their own choice about any topic or experience under the sun.

She felt the continued practice in self-expression would unleash the creative wellsprings and build self-confidence in verbal skills. She has not altered those convictions, but now she has cut the exercise to a weekly project. The pupils and their parents feel, she explains, that vocabulary lessons carry a higher premium these days. Although the daily writing assignment may have done more in the long run to build verbal skills, it was curtailed because short-range goals have come to carry greater weight in the minds of scores of taxpayers and school officials.

Mass, Chrome, and Marketing

A critical danger of adopting short-range educational goals as prime targets lies in the tendency to devote greater attention to pupils en masse than to pupils as individual entities. The pit is an easy one in which to fall, because all pupils share certain common learning needs. In the race for short-range proof of educational superiority, the teacher who dares to develop the idiosyncratic feels she may be lost come tenure time.

An equally pernicious aspect of anxiety fallout in the public school is the temptation to emphasize the chrome of education at the sacrifice of tuning up the machinery under the hood. Reacting to public pressure for new ideas, many administrators have become easy game for the salesmen of brave new teaching machines, evaluations on punch cards, and all manner of brightly packaged test kits. Many of these are so new they haven't been properly tested or validated. A teaching machine may be no better than the program fed into it, but to an anxiety-ridden school official or worried parent, it may appear to be the pot of gold at the rainbow's end.

Perhaps the most tragic symptom of anxiety on the school scene is the tendency of pupils to plan their educational futures in the manner of junior account executives plotting a campaign for increased celery sales.

"How can I make myself more marketable to the Ivy League colleges?" the pupil may wonder under the weight of increasing talk about college competition and overcrowding. "What gut courses are available? What activities will look best on my record? What ministers have the biggest prestige value on application recommendations? What tutors do the best coaching job for the College Board tests?"

No Pink Pills

There just isn't any pink pill that the public school can swallow to recover from the fallout effects. I have the uncomfortable intuition that we will be living with them for some time to come. However, as in combatting any psychological malaise, the first step forward lies in confronting reality. For almost four years we have tended to assume that the disturbance was exclusively external in nature. My observations, gleaned from experience as a psychologist in the public schools during that period, suggest a contrary finding.

When we realized that the new Soviet education had made certain striking advances over our own, we first tried to modify our educational products while we scurried about flipping switches and searching for panaceas in the desperate hope of reasserting our superiority overnight. In some cases, as in Rickover's dramatic proposals, a willingness was expressed to scrap the traditional machinery itself.

Perhaps the reaffirmation of our democratic ideology will not come of its own accord. It would be wrong to assume that the education profession is apart rather than a part of the national population, that we school people are immune to our country's general anxieties. On the other hand, our professional image suggests the desirability of public leadership. Do we dare, in an era of power psychology, to reassert the values of individual discovery and development? Or will we postpone that task in favor of mass-producing a new generation of competitively designed and competitively operated, acquisitively oreinted and security-starved cold war graduates?

ROBERT L. SHANNON

The Numbers Racket in Education

A digital nightmare is successfully subverting the aims of education in the United States. With equal enthusiasm, economy-minded legislators and altruistic agencies are subsidizing this subversion which is so subtle that neither the victims nor the perpetrators realize what is happening. Educators are buying a plan that threatens to undermine their very existence.

Education is a human-centered concept: schools, colleges, and universities are created to nurture the potentialities of the individual student. The accepted aims of education are to involve students in the quest for truth, to expand their understandings, to lead them to reexamine their beliefs, to help them to discover the significance of self, and to induce them to participate actively in personally significant scholarly endeavors. That an astonishingly small proportion of the student population actually experiences fulfillment of these aims is not the fault of the students. The campus bookies who manipulate vast assortments of digits in endless combinations are dictating the style and duration of the undergraduate's college experience.

Securely entrenched in the academic community is a vast army of scorekeepers who calculate the life chances of each student and categorize him in relation to one of a million inconsequential norms: whether a student is "in," "on warning," "on probation," or "pregnant" is cranked out by a multitude of odds-making machines on college campuses. Grade-point ratios, quality points, honor points, upper division demands, professional school requisites, scores on course examinations, hearing scores—the list is without end—all combine to become the dominating influences in the life of today's college student. Conversations between students are seldom about ideas. The talk centers instead around where the professor struck the curve, what proportion failed the test, what averages they have as they enter the final examination, or who looms as the grade getter in the class. Possibilities for pari-mutuel betting on the collegiate horse

Robert L. Shannon, "The Numbers Racket in Higher Education," *The Journal of Teacher Education*, 18, no. 1 (Spring, 1967). Published by the National Commission on Teacher Education and Professional Standards, National Education Association.

races might represent a whole new revenue source for an enterprising administrator; a cash dividend could be an unforeseen concomitant that might accrue from the dedication to digits instead of to students.

Pouring in data that scale the undergraduate in every category from IQ to sex appeal, the psychometricians or evaluation services or some such group will extract from their machines a verdict by way of the appropriate form letter addressed to a student number. This letter might announce that the student is to be graduated with honors, dismissed from further study for a probationary period, or permitted to continue his anonymous process of collecting points, credits, and course numbers until a sufficient quantity is garnered to make him eligible for a nameless bachelor's degree which he will receive along with thousands of identical peers in a mass pronouncement by a college dean he has never met.

Sheri is one of these undergraduates. Coming to my office for counsel, she described her plight:

> You know, I need a 2.0 grade-point average to stay in school. I've completed 96 hours of college work, and my grade-point average is 1.906. Right now I'm enrolled in 6 hours of classes. Now, remember that I was on final academic warning the trimester before because I made only a 1.85 GPA. The next trimester, I raised it to a 1.98—still less than 2.0 overall—so that meant final warning status. The following semester, I did fairly well in everything but history. You might know I'd get that history professor who was so unhappy. It turned out that his wife was divorcing him—you know the stories about how he came to class sort of drunk. He left the campus after that trimester. What a mess! Anyway, his grades stuck, and mine was F. This took me below a 2.0 overall, and I had to stay out of school for a trimester, during which I worked at the hospital. There, they seemed to think I was all right. Well, when I got back into school after petitioning to the Academic Policies Committee, I raised my overall GPA above 2.0. This took me off final warning—sort of. I mean, if I fall below a 2.0 GPA, I'm to be kicked out of school for good, and I'm a senior now with 96 credits finished out of 120 I need to graduate. Well, this gets me to my problem. I'm scared—and here's why.
>
> After 96 hours, my overall GPA is 1.906. I am now taking two courses for 6 credits. If I divide 3 into the total number of hours, I get the number of units. Then I multiply by 6, because 6 points equal 3 credits with a grade of C, and in this way, I determine the minimum number of honor points I need to get a C grade. Then I add up the grades I have, using the base point of 165 honor points that I have after completing 90 hours. In addition, I took 6 hours the first half of summer school and made an A and a C, which equal 12 honor points plus 6. This increased my honor points by 18.

Now I'm taking 6 hours (two courses) and earning a B+ in one and a D+ in the other. If I drop the one in which I have a D+, I'll be 3 honor points low and be forced to drop out of college permanently (at least from this school). I must make a B in one and an A in the other, and then I'll just have the required 2.00 overall GPA to stay in school for the two more trimesters I need before graduating; the A and B will give me the 204 honor points I need to be permitted to remain. I just don't understand why all of these honor points and grade-point averages should decide my whole life.

On frequent occasions, the same young lady, obviously not a great grade getter—perhaps not even a scholar—has been in my office to discuss her digital dilemma. Seldom have the conversations been about an exciting idea, a book, or a visiting lecturer she found provocative. Inevitably, these meetings have been devoted to the kind of juggling she must do to beat the numbers game into which the university has forced her.

Sufficient faculty and money are available to implement alternatives that can reverse the trend toward a depersonalized education. However, the situation is so firmly established that changes will demand the type of bold administrative decisions college administrators are reluctant to make. As long as appeasement of the vested interests is the theme among university administrators, this disease will continue its epidemic inroads on formal education.

Educators have some choices to make. Technology is a potential key to deep personal involvement in education. As Marshall McLuhan wrote in *Understanding Media*, "The social and educational patterns latent in automation are those of self-employment and artistic autonomy."* What a tragedy that people in higher education elect to negotiate this subversion via computer rather than to utilize all dimensions of technology to augment students' personalized scholarly endeavors!

The quest must be for arrangements that enable the institutions to provide a personalized educational program, with technology and research complementing human relations with students instead of negating this primary dimension of higher education. If the plans and programs do not serve the individual educational requirements of the students who *choose* to attend a particular college or university, then these plans and programs are subverting the intentions of the school, the society, and the students.

American education can accommodate the masses. Today, because a college education is in such demand, the admissions situation has shifted from a buyers' to a sellers' market. In some instances, this has become an excuse for poor teaching; in others, it has given rise to mass calcula-

---

* Marshall McLuhan, *Understanding Media: The Extensions of Man*, Toronto, McGraw-Hill Company of Canada, 1964, p. 359.

tions of student achievements which yield whatever biases the controllers of machines tend to favor.

Punchboards have been illegal for many years because it was decided that the detrimental effects of gambling could thereby be decreased. Today's punchboard is the college student. Perhaps federal legislation will be necessary to eliminate the tendency to "make book" on the educational experiences and probabilities of college students.

Such a condition is unnecessary. Other plans for higher education are possible at no greater cost. Unless educators force the digits to serve human purposes, the systems will eventually make a farce of a great opportunity to create programs of higher education that will produce the most enlightened, education-oriented society in the world. Education is a subjective affair; sweeping students in or out of the college environment by objective means is intolerable. Policies relating to educational decisions must conform to a subjective interpretation of their validity as applied to individual students. The essential is to look at the individual student as a person, not as a possessor of digits.

The student is the important subject, an individual with idiosyncracies to be cherished; he cannot be treated as a punchboard whose primary function is to appear on a normal curve or a distribution chart. Positive alternatives to the numbers game do exist for those college and university persons who comprehend their functions.

NORMAN COUSINS

Not So Fast

The ultimate test of education is represented by the ability to think. We are not talking about casual or random thought. We are talking about sequential thought, that is, the process by which one frame of ideas is attached to another in workable order so that they fit together without rattling or falling apart the moment they come in contact with a logical objection or query.

Sequential thought is the most difficult work in the entire range of human effort. Even when undertaken by a highly trained intelligence, it can be enormously fatiguing. When attempted by untrained minds, it can produce total exhaustion within a matter of minutes, sometimes seconds. For it requires an almost limitless number of mental operations. The route must be anticipated between the present location of an idea and where it is supposed to go. Memory must be raked for relevant material. Facts or notions must be sorted out, put in their proper places, then supplied with connective tissue. Then comes the problem of weighing and emphasis.

Sequential thought, like any other advanced form of human activity, is the result of systematic training. Just sitting in front of television screen watching baseball games for a dozen years or more doesn't automatically qualify a man to throw strikes with blazing speed. Either he has the educated muscles to pitch or he hasn't. The same is true of thought. A man who doesn't know how to use the muscles of his intelligence can hardly be expected to cope with a problem requiring concentration and the ability to think abstractly.

How, then, can a person be taught to think sequentially? It isn't necessary to devise special courses of study for this purpose. All that is necessary is for existing courses to foster those conditions that promote proper habits of thought. The problem lies not with the curriculum; it lies rather with the way education is generally organized.

Fragmentation is the enemy of sequential thought. Yet there is a large degree of fragmentation in the way a youngster is called upon to meet his

Norman Cousins, "Not So Fast," *Saturday Review*, July 6, 1963.

educational obligations. He may have four or five different courses of study. In the space of a few hours he has to shift his focus of attention drastically several times, resulting often in a blurring of the significance of what he is being taught. Each class or course tends to be something of a universe in itself. This may provide welcome relief in some cases but it also violates many of the basic laws of concentration as they apply to intellectual absorption and retention. This is hardly reassuring at a time when the relationships among the various fields of learning have become a prime need in education.

Homework assignments are only rarely correlated. On some nights a student may have three or four major assignments, making it virtually impossible to do them all adequately. We have never been able to understand why a homework paper in history, say, and an assignment in English composition cannot be combined. Far better to give a youngster a chance to put his history paper into decent English than to require him to go racing through separate assignments in both subjects. More basic still: why shouldn't the school attempt some measure of coordination in homework assignments, with each course having at least one night a week in which genuine concentration and sustained work would be expected and made possible?

H. S. F. Helmholtz, the noted German physicist who died thirty years ago, described three principal stages in effective thinking. In the first stage, a problem is carefully examined in all its aspects and all directions. In the second stage, ample time is allowed for a problem or an idea to get through to the subconscious in order that the mind may work on it and develop it even when not specifically focused on it. The third stage involves the conditions or circumstances under which an idea is brought to full term and makes its appearance. Helmholtz's analysis may not hold for all people—nothing is more individualistic than a man's thoughts—but at least he emphasizes the need for thought about thinking. Most of our confusion, James Harvey Robinson once wrote, comes from this failure to give thought to thought.

If we are to help Johnny to think—which is to say, we are to help him become truly educated—it becomes necessary to respect the natural requirements of thought. Somewhere along the line in recent years, a speed-up has taken place in large areas of education. Johnny is expected to read faster, study faster, write faster, and think faster. No doubt, this is less the fault of educators than of the world itself. But the problems posed by an Age of Speed are not met by snap judgments, one-page memos on complex subjects, lightning-fast reading techniques, or rapid writing. We meet our problems only as we comprehend them and give them sustained and sequential thought. The quickest way to compound these problems is to put them in a pressure cooker.

––––––––––––––

"It is a tradition here not to walk on the grass. This tradition goes into effect at noon today."

Sign on a Midwestern College Campus

ROBERT L. SHANNON

Who Failed, Student or School?

Is it possible that those who succeed in school are the poor thinkers and the grade grubbers? The list of creative, brilliant people who have made a significant "breakthrough" in some field by innovating, persevering, or extending an idea has an astonishing parallel. The parallel is that in many cases these individuals were perceived by their teachers as poor students. Frequently they were failures in the school setting.

Buckminster Fuller, creator of the geodesic dome, has revolutionized architecture. He has pulled together many diverse technological discoveries and used them to improve the lives of people. He attended Harvard on two occasions: he was a dropout, and once he was thrown out for "general irresponsibility." Many years later he was invited back to Harvard as a visiting lecturer. Fuller refers to himself as a "random element."

Truman Capote, successful novelist (*In Cold Blood*), never finished high school. "I was never any good at school," he recalls. "I hated it. I'd been writing for three years, and to me it was no joke. The principal of that school hated me, he wanted to throw me out. But I had a teacher at that school, a wonderful lady, who was my greatest sort of champion." When asked about Mr. Capote the teacher said, "You just had to understand that Truman wasn't going to do the regular thing."

W. C. Fields, comedian, juggler, writer, is said to have attended school about four years. The figure may be a little high. One of his relatives believed that he turned up for school one Monday in the autumn of his sixth year but that he lasted only till around noon. Indications were that he found the classroom cramped and the teacher's manner inadequate. He told others that he taught himself to read. Fields became a knowledgeable scholar in English literature. He totally rejected the regimentation of school as a place to get an education.

Oscar-winner *Ed Begley* never finished grammar school. Why? "It wasn't because I was a wild kid or because I had terrible grades. I just found working at anything connected with the theater more interesting than going to school." Recently Mr. Begley was invited to be guest lecturer in drama at Syracuse University.

One of *Thomas Edison's* grade-school teachers wrote his mother that he should be switched to remedial school because he was inattentive, indolent, and his brain was seriously "addled."

Louis Pasteur had his parents in despair. All he ever did was go fishing. He didn't study science until he was in his twenties.

Bear Bryant, regarded by many as the most successful and controversial college football coach in the nation has said about himself: "I wasn't very smart in school, and lazy to boot. Of all the people who might do something in life I was the one folks figured would do the least. I was always involved in something."

The parents of *Albert Einstein* worried that he was seriously stupid because he couldn't speak until he was over three. At twenty he got a job as an office worker and spent a lot of time scribbling mathematical doodles. At thirty his doodles caught on in the world of science.

Adlai Stevenson was such a mediocre student in high school that he had to be sent to a prep school before being admitted to Princeton.

Winston Churchill was regarded by his teachers as a very poor student. Late in his life he said, "I am surprised that in later life I became so experienced at taking degrees, when as a schoolboy I was so bad at passing examinations. In fact, one might say that no one ever passed so few examinations and received so many degrees."

When *Peter Ustinov* was a schoolboy, he received a teacher's report which read, "He has great originality—which must be curbed at all costs." He sold his first essay at the age of 14. Since then he has written eighteen plays, seven movies (directing and coproducing six), has had featured roles in nineteen movies, and has won two academy awards. His short stories have been published in *The Atlantic Monthly,* and, most recently, he sold his first painting (for $75).

Education Is No Parenthesis ()

Several years ago the eminent educator, Harold Benjamin, wrote a little book with the title, *The Saber-Tooth Curriculum,* which made a caricature of an educational system which held the popular philosophy that education of the young should be concerned only with the handing down to them a body of fundamental, ready-made knowledge consisting of eternal truths, valid in all times and places. In this book the new generations were taught the skills which had been needed by their forebears to protect themselves from the saber-tooth tiger. Because of climatic changes accompanying the Great Glacier the tiger became extinct. Unfortunately the curriculum, which was based on the problems related to the extinct tiger, lived on.

Benjamin was saying that while it may be necessary to pass some ready-made solutions along to the oncoming generations, such information and knowledge to be valid must have reference to the problems that were their source. Most of all he was pointing to the need of inducting the young into the spirit and problems of their own society. He was not arguing for the narrow "presentism" which is the hallmark of a shallow and popular cult which is always promoted by the "practical man" of every age. He recognized that a curriculum grounded on such immediacy would be as weak as one based on the philosophy which has as its only ingredients eternal and absolute truths. Just as he did not believe in living in the past, the author of *The Saber-Tooth Curriculum* also opposed "postponed living"—living not for this world or living for a future day in which all difficulties would be completely resolved.

Those who would devise a curriculum which will meet the challenges of today must realize that the problems of the present have their roots in the relevant past, and the significance of the problems cannot be really grappled with unless there is a thorough examination of these roots. The fact that history cannot be relied upon always to repeat itself does not change the fact that, if properly utilized, it can be a necessary instrument in the search for the elusive truths of today and the uncertain trends for tomorrow. What is relevant to life today and tomorrow needs to be taught no matter from what age it comes.

For a curriculum to be relevant for today and tomorrow, it must be based on the principle that theory has a decisive function in the education program. It should be recognized that the only difference between the person who believes in theory and the one who does not is that the latter acts on the basis of a theory just as does the former, but he does not recognize nor understand his own theory. . . . Good theory then is good vision. We need better educational theory today if we are to have better educational practice tomorrow.

E. E. Cummings says in one of his poems, "Life's not a paragraph and death I think is no parenthesis." The poet might have meant that death is no interlude, no interval. His words could be interpreted to mean that death is not something which is separated from life, like a word in a parenthesis (death) separated from the flow of a sentence. Whether this is the interpretation meant by the poet is not too important for the development of our idea here, but it is important to make the point that those seeking to devise a curriculum for students in today's world should not make it like something parenthetical which is added and is not central. Good theory can keep education central to life and from becoming isolated and unrelated to it. But most important of all it must be remembered by those who shape America's educational programs that life is ongoing and never static and education represents life and not the type of death that means finality.

J. A. BATTLE

The Education We Need Today and Why We Need It

I heard the story recently of an African lion who was determined that he be recognized as the King of the Jungle. He walked up to the crocodile, slapped him on the tail, and said, "Hello, Lizard. Who is King of the Jungle?" "You, Sir Lion," said the lizard. Then the lion hit the hippopotamus on the hips and asked, "Fatso, who is King of the Jungle?" The hippopotamus meekly replied, "Sir Lion, you're the King of the Jungle." The lion slapped the elephant on his hind legs and asked him, "Big Boy, who is King of the Jungle?" but the elephant paid him no attention and kept on chewing leaves. The lion went around to the front and hit the elephant on his front legs and demanded, "Who is the King of the Jungle?" but the elephant still went on chewing leaves. So the lion jumped up and hit the elephant on a more sensitive spot, his ear. The elephant stopped eating, picked up the lion in his trunk, swung him around over his head a few times, and threw him against a nearby tree. The lion, almost completely dazed, opened one eye slightly and with great effort lifted up his head a few inches and plaintively squeaked out. "Well, you needn't get so upset just because you don't know the answer."

The problem in education today is not that the answers to the questions being asked are unknown but that the wrong questions are being asked. Too many of the questions are based on old shibboleths that have little relevance to a society dominated by technology. This is even true in teacher education where some professors are spending their time in class asking questions about Bestor and Rickover of teachers-to-be who will soon be swamped by the products of IBM and may never again hear of those two men. However, the professors continue to deliver the same funny remarks, such as the one about an Admiral going on a submarine trip to Switzerland, that they heard delivered by their own graduate professors. Thus they give Bestor and Rickover continuous resuscitation.

The excellent teacher does not isolate himself from reality. It is most important that he possess good theory, but how is he to know whether it is good or bad if it is never tested against reality? "The supreme misfortune," said Leonardo da Vinci, "is when theory outstrips performance." A more serious misfortune is when theory has no relevance to life Too many theoreticians who are today designing irrelevant theories for education attempt to defend themselves by claiming that those who oppose their poor theories are against theory in general. When one couples poor theory with great self-confidence one is headed for a great disaster such as befell Major General Edward Braddock in 1755. Braddock's parade ground theories did not keep his mighty force from meeting disaster at the hands of a band of Indian warriors who had never seen a military parade ground. After his defeat Braddock said, "We shall know how to deal with them another time." But there was no "another time" for Braddock because two days later he died of his wounds and was buried by George Washington "in the road near the head of the column" of the retreating forces so that the Indians would not find his grave. Washington, who was an aide to Braddock on the advance to Fort Du Quesne, wrote soon after the defeat, "We have been most scandalously beaten by a trifling body of men." One of the principal criticisms made of Braddock's management of the campaign was that he "displayed over-confidence in a type of warfare with which he was unfamiliar."

General Braddock did not make himself familiar with the type of warfare he was forced to wage, and the same is true of many theorists in both politics and education today. This is why the present war on poverty is being fought as if the conditions were the same as in the 1930s when the manufacture of goods was far more dependent on manpower than in this day of automation and cybernation. Yet it should be noted that some of those who are opposing the war on poverty "as a matter of principle" are not doing so on the basis of knowledge they have about 1967, but on the basis of knowledge they have about the 1920s.

Anyone who claims that American education in the 1960s is poorer than it was in the past just doesn't know about education in the past. There is more educational excellence in one state today than there was in all of the states in the Union just a few decades ago. But the problem today is not concerned with whether education today is better or worse than in the past, but how it is different. The question that needs to be asked is, "Is American education relevant to the latter part of the twentieth century?" To be judged relevant it must exhibit a deep concern for solving the great problems of a society that is dominated by technology. Frankly, I have not discovered this deep concern.

Lamenting about this age of technology is not going to help modern man to live a finer life nor is just talking in clichés about man being the master instead of the servant of technology. How education is going on in the same old way, teaching its irrelevant subject matter, was demonstrated to me most vividly recently when I tried to find some liberal arts faculty members to join together as humanists, scientists, and social scientists in a teaching project that has "The City" as its theme. I heard the disdainful refrain over and over again, "I'm a chemist, I don't know anything about urban problems" and "I'm a historian, I don't know anything about urban problems." It is not so frightening that these university professors do not know anything about urban problems, but what is frightening is their lack of a desire to learn about them and their attitude that such problems have no relationship to their subjects.

Today 70 percent of the American population lives in urban communities, and it is predicted that within a short time that figure will increase to 80 percent. Yet, American politics and education, despite some recent progress, are still oriented toward nontechnical and rural living. Many politicians talk nostalgically of the rural past. Many of the elementary school textbooks from which our children learn to read are illustrated by pictures, with which the young urban learner is supposed to identify, of children growing up in rural areas or in small towns in which the father walks to work and the mother talks to the neighbors over her white picket fence. Pictures representing a culture other than that of the child serve a useful educational purpose. But since these illustrations are supposed to represent his own culture, it is no wonder that the child may believe that he knows more about the present world than the authors of his textbooks. Certainly he knows more about the space program than most of his teachers. And it wasn't from educational television that he learned about the exciting exploits in space and the dangers faced by our astronauts. It was from commercial television. With the leaders of our educational and political life giving so little attention to the serious problems created by technology it is no wonder that our society is running amuck, seemedly possessed with a homicidal mania.

Despite, or possibly because of, the torrential flood of new knowledge in the last few years, wholesome happiness in the lives of our school pupils (and perhaps in the lives of their teachers and parents) seems to be decreasing. Americans in their twin pursuit of more knowledge and faster living may be losing their true happiness. Except for the "liberty" part, it is rather unfashionable to mention today that our Declaration of Independence states that the members of the human family "are endowed by their Creator with certain inalienable rights, that among them are life, liberty, and the pursuit of happiness." While the American school today is finding it difficult to make much headway in the teaching of human happiness, its failure in this is simply the failure of the total American society. This is a society that has become so enamored with science and technology that it is becoming the slave of science and technology rather than the reverse being true. Our society has almost completely ignored the warning of one of the greatest of our scientists, Albert Einstein, when he said, "Politics are more difficult than physics and the world is more apt to die from bad politics than from bad physics."

We are living in an age that is much loved by science fiction writers and junk dealers and in general is abhorred by the intellectual. The intellectual and the machine have simply not come to terms with each other. Yet because of the machine this is the first age in history in which a large proportion of the members of the human family have time for intellectual pursuits. The machine is also creating a need for more people today to have a greater amount of education than has been needed in any previous age in the history of man. The present-day intellectual would be a more responsible person if he did not attempt to be a member of an exclusive class but instead encouraged all the members of our democratic society to join him in striving to gain more intellectual interests.

Both the educator and the lay citizen recognize that in our present society there is a need for more education than ever before, but they do not seem to understand that the type of education needed must be different from any education known before. This lack of understanding is endangering the foundations of modern society. If this society is to be a healthy one, it must be understood that today the welfare of the human spirit is dependent upon relating education to space travel, urbanization, the communications media, nuclear energy, cybernation, and now unmined resources of the oceans.

As teachers it is our responsibility to help our students to think and act as total human beings on the great problems of present-day life. If we teach our students only to cope with fragmented "busy work" assignments in which they are required to find the old answers in the back of the book or the new answers to the "new mathematics" or "new physics" unrelated to the real problems of our times, many of these students will continue to become alienated from our society.

Today the American child is being drowned in knowledge, new and old. When he most needs a lifeline to keep from sinking in this "raw" knowledge, he is given still more "raw" knowledge. Instead of only handing out more knowledge it is our task as teachers to help the young to integrate knowledge with values, thought, and behavior. Only when there is such an integration will education be made relevant to life. To offer educational programs that are irrelevant to life is to reduce education to an absurdity.

The school and the college have not assumed enough of the intellectual responsibility for relating science and technology to the pursuit of happiness, health, and human dignity, and they seem all too willing to leave to commercial television much of the task of teaching the potentialities and problems related to science and technology to pupils who are not specializing in these areas. It is no wonder that many American young people are increasingly becoming alienated from their society. After all, what they see on the surface strongly indicates that the human spirit and the human graces have been replaced by the robot and there is nothing that they can do about it.

Although Norman Cousins, the editor of *Saturday Review*, is probably more concerned about war and peace than any other problem of our age, he is also deeply concerned about our environmental problems. He recently wrote:

> The American people are involved in a war far more deadly than the war in Vietnam, but very few of them seem aware of it; even fewer are doing anything about it. The war is being waged against the environment. Land, air and water are the basics of that environment. All these basics are under unremitting attack. . . .
>
> The human race may not be tied together politically or philosophically or culturally, but the one thing that all the world's people have in common is a finite amount of land, an air envelope that is rapidly filling up with filth and poisons, and an uneven water supply that is largely unprotected against infection by sewage and noxious wastes.
>
> The human intelligence that created industrial civilization now has the assignment of making that civilization compatible with man's basic needs. If this is not done, the verdict on man is likely to be that he is first of all an anti-environment predator and a producer of garbage and poisons, and only secondarily a creator of fine works, great deeds, and beauty.*

While education is the key to our making life even better here on earth, education means different things to different people. But if it is to mean anything of significance, it must be viewed as an enterprise that has a deep commitment, to use the words of William Faulkner upon his receiving the Nobel Prize, "to help man endure by lifting his heart."

Today the individual in our complex society has little choice whether to use or not to use technology. It permeates his life, whether he likes it or not. Yet despite the fact that it is such a powerful force, it need not be one that takes away his individuality and human dignity. It could enhance these virtues, but for it to do so, the educator who values the finer qualities in our society must move now, in the words of Marshall McLuhan, "from the ivory tower to the control tower of society."

In our technological society there is a tendency to underestimate

* Norman Cousins, "The Other War," *Saturday Review*, June 18, 1966, p. 26.

knowledge concerning human beings that may be just as true as any principles in physics. I am sure that all of my readers are familiar with the famous study of the human factor in industrial productivity made a number of years ago at the Hawthorne Plant of the Western Electric Company near Chicago. The experiment revealed what seemed to be a mysterious effect. No matter how the physical working conditions of the employees were altered, whether they were improved or made worse, the employees taking part in the experiment worked more effectively. Productivity increased no matter what the working conditions because the workers were stimulated by being in the experiment. This point is now well recognized, but most people still seem to miss another implication of the study: when people are encouraged to enlist their energies in a process of self-discovery the increase in efficiency is phenomenal.

The education we need today would combine a fine system of values with modern technology. In a recent editorial in *Saturday Review* entitled "The Computer and the Poet" Cousins wrote:

> The computer makes possible a phenomenal leap in human proficiency; it demolishes the fences around the practical and even the theoretical intelligence. But the question persists and indeed grows whether the computer will make it harder or easier for human beings to know who they really are, to identify their real problems, to respond more fully to beauty, to place adequate value on life, and to make their world safer than it now is.
>
> The biggest single need in computer technology is not for improved circuitry, or enlarged capacity, or prolonged memory, or miniaturized containers, but for better questions and better use of the answers. Without taking anything away from the technicians, we think it might be fruitful to effect some sort of junction between the computer technologist and the poet.*

Mr. Cousins makes an excellent point, but we know enough about the problems of our society and the processes that have to be initiated to solve them to be more precise in defining the type of "junction" that is needed. Cousins' "some sort of junction" and C. P. Snow's "communication" between the "two cultures" may provide much needed inspiration, but neither is exact enough to make a great difference in practice. In the world of action the arts and the sciences can and must each begin to view life as a whole and then together begin to attack the environmental problems of our world, not piecemeal but in their totality.

The place for the arts and sciences to begin a significant joint venture

---

* Norman Cousins, "The Computer and the Poet," *Saturday Review*, July 23, 1966, p. 42.

concerned with life as a whole is the American school. Those who will be in charge of the age of cybernetics, for instance, are the school pupils of today. What better group to work with is there for an educational team composed of scholars in the arts and sciences.

Dr. Kenneth Boulding, an economics professor at the University of Michigan, has compared the earth to a manned spaceship going through space and time with a limited store of resources on board and receiving a circumscribed input of energy from the sun. The permissible rate of consumption for maintaining life of the occupants aboard obviously cannot exceed the regenerative capacity of the spaceship. Men must achieve a more rational and a more balanced state of life in which pollution is matched by purification and consumption is matched by replenishment of resources. Professor Boulding's analogy could serve as an indication of what the computer technologist, the scientist, and the poet might do for the urban school. They could help the urban school to relate better to the problems of its environment and thus to serve its society better.

If the educational lock step is to be broken and American children are to learn how to cope with and improve upon the world they *are* living in and the world they *will* be living in, a dramatic departure from current educational practices must be taken. It is somewhat doubtful that the ills of the school can be cured when dismal and chronic social conditions sicken the remainder of the society of which it is a part. If it is almost impossible for a school system to be healthier than the society it serves, then what may be needed is all-out, simultaneous attack upon the ills of the society and the curriculum of the school.

A workable approach—as a first step—to resolve the desperate plight of the American city and its school system is to set up one model urban school system with a curriculum geared to help its pupils to learn how to think about and cope with the problems of their urban community. The community could be utilized as a laboratory in which the pupils seek solutions to the value-laden problems concerned with conformity, impersonalization, and dependence and to specific urban problems which affect their lives, such as de facto segregation, crime, traffic congestion, family disunity, sanitation, pollution of air and water, aesthetic poverty, crowded housing conditions, and poor cultural and recreational programs. As background study for solving these great urban problems the school curriculum could include studies of such topics as industrialization, mass media, cybernation, atomic energy, conservation, ecology, crime, space, transportation, and racial integration, and such academic subjects as literature, music, art, physics, chemistry, biology, sociology, anthropology, American and European history, political science, and mathematics.

The purpose of such a curriculum would be to help the pupils of the school to learn to think about and act upon problems relevant to their present lives and to prepare them to deal with the serious problems of urban living as adults.

The urban public school is doing a creditable job now in educating the children of the middle class but it is inadequate to carry the greater burden of health and socioeconomic reform and integration for the poor. If an attack were to be made on the problems of an urban community at the same time that a relevant curriculum was being developed in the community's school system, real solutions might be originated for the overburdened society of the city. In such a joint attack some of the older pupils of the school could serve as junior members of task forces working directly on the urban problems. This would be invaluable educational experience and it would also help to get the support of parents for the work of the task forces. Almost all pupils of the school could serve as members of task forces concerned with the school itself and most of these problems would be related to those of the urban community at large.

In the proposed curriculum for the urban school the pupils would study the sciences, humanities, and social sciences in relation to the problems of modern man in an urban society that is to a great extent dominated by the atom and the computer. This study would be a positive answer to the question "Will it help to make life more livable on earth and man more humane?" A major aim of such a curriculum would be to learn how independence and individuality can be retained in an increasingly more technological society. With this approach instead of two academic worlds which are disjointed, not communicating with each other, or, worse still, irrelevant to life, there would be one academic world with the sciences, humanities, and social sciences joined together as equal partners in a common cause: a search for the old ideals of truth, beauty, and goodness through modern means for the modern world.

MARSHALL McLUHAN

The New Education

Marshall McLuhan's observations on the mass media of our century, their many problems and advantages, have almost become part of our thinking. His two most influential books, The Gutenburg Galaxy *and* Understanding Media, *are the best treatments of modern communication problems in print, while his year-long study of education for the United States Government is still causing reverberations along educational corridors. Because it was the most comfortable medium to work in, his views on the present and future state of education were sought out in a taped interview for reproduction here.*

Q. *What in your opinion is happening in education today?*

A good point to begin with, when talking about education, is the Destination Syndrome. Goals are disappearing today, because we cannot maintain a point of view at very high speeds. We have an environment that is moving at very fast speeds. The speed of information movement is very high and it creates a field rather than a simple area of subjects; it does not create subjects, it creates total field. This is in one way ecumenism, as opposed to the old sectarian, fragmented setup. And the same result is being felt in the area of subjects in the schools. They feel more and more need to interrelate and dialogue among themselves.

Q. *In view of this Destination Syndrome, how is the computer affecting education?*

The computer in education is in a very tentative state but it does represent basically speeded up access to information, and when it is applied to the telephone and to Xerox it permits access to the libraries of the world, or to information in any part of the world, almost immediately, without delay. And so the immediate effect of the computer is to pull up the walls of the subjects and divisions of knowledge in favor of over-all field, total awareness—*Gestalt*. Kids are already perfectly familiar with this approach in the entertainment field; it is not an area of subjects, or areas, or wall,

Marshall McLuhan, "The New Education," *The Basilian Teacher*, 11, no. 2 (February, 1967). Produced from a taped interview with Mr. McLuhan.

but anything. It is under the earth, or on the moon, or in any part of the globe simultaneously.

Q. You have written extensively about the "global village." What effect is this having on the young people today?

They take it for granted. The Peace Corps itself is part of that development. Kids are prepared to go to any any part of the world at the drop of a hat, settle down and learn the language, learn everything. They take that for granted, they also find it very congenial, because it is a kind of crash-programming. The great appeal of the Peace Corps is crash-programming. You do nothing but learn that language day and night. When you move into a new area, a new territory and learn a new language, the language is not a new subject, it is an environment, it is total. This is the pattern of learning in the future. Learning of the future is going to be by way of environment—total. And that means accelerated and indefinite. Up to now we have tended to classify things, and separate them from each other as much as possible, learning them one at a time, not all together, as they exist in the environment.

The way a child learns its mother tongue is to use every gesture, every intonation, every sound, as a new experience. It is not a classified experience, it is a probe, an instrument in his hands for probing the world; it is total. And so the learning of the mother tongue is at very high speed. By the age of two the child has pretty well got it. There is no existing method of education which could teach anybody that much in that time. I think we are going to devise ways for extending that kind of learning to every form of human learning. It means using all the senses at once, involving oneself totally in the situation as a way of learning.

Q. Do you think the teach-in is a new form of learning?

This is a form in which the student body is involved in the process. They are not just on the receiving end. The student or learner takes on a much more active role. Just as in the modern theater the audience is increasingly active—the new theater of this century puts the audience on the stage, in the play. The Peace Corps, too, could be considered as participated democracy in this way. Even the Company of Young Canadians is working along this line—the kids become totally involved in problem solving, in the really difficult situations. That is really what they want. They want learning through things that the adults do not know. They do not want to match their wits against the teacher's wits on things that are already known. They increasingly want to involve themselves in discovery, problem solving, and action. You know the new word is: "This is where the action is!"

Q. What does this mean for the teacher?

The teacher has to get more students involved in the teaching process, in other words, learning, discovery, etc. The teacher has to become more and more involved in the problems of the students. In other words the tutorial dialogue is coming back into the learning process.

There is a book called *The Imperial Intellect,* by Dwight Culler, about Cardinal Newman when he was a young professor at Oxford. Newman began an educational revolution there, which came off; he brought it off; he fought furiously for it—it was the tutorial system. The tutorial system did not exist at Oxford until his time. What he said was this: instead of lecturing to these people, let us use the cram-coach procedure that exists in this town for the privileged and wealthy students. Let us bring it inside the college. The cram-coach is a highly paid crammer brought in as a tutor. Now the characteristic about the cram-coach system that Newman admired was that it taught everything at once; it did not teach one subject at a time. You paid a higher fee and you learned everything at once—now that is dialogue; that is tutorial, as opposed to a system of lectures.

Now in our time we are trying to extend this tutorial system by electric means, by programmed instruction of various kinds. We are trying to extend it democratically to everybody. We are trying to. But some are mostly still trying to put the old teaching into the new instrument. This is what they are trying to do in university organized teach-ins, that is programming—hoping to enlarge the teaching process by accepting "hot" material like the newspaper. Taking "hot" issues in a teach-in is a way of artificial respiration for the old educational corpse.

The new information environment that we live in has a delayed feedback, a sort of double-take recognition. You stop in your tracks, take another look—recognition. The double-take is a very curious instance of the power of recognition. In a highly visual culture we think of the double-take only in visual things, but it is part of our learning make-up also. The only way you really learn anything is by being startled into recognition. This new process, the tutorial, is being extended through the whole environment, in the sense that the environment itself is charged with information today; this is a sort of teaching machine. The environment is increasingly programmed, and programmed much more richly than any classroom ever was. Now I think that this might not be a bad theme to meditate upon: that for the first time in human history the outside environment is richer than the inside classroom. This never happened before as far as I know. Always in the past the inside classroom situation was richer than the ordinary environment of that time.

There is a book called *Classroom and the Factory,* by Clark and Sloan, in which the authors attempt to estimate how much time and money are spent by companies on this continent in education on company time. They estimate that the budget of such teaching and study on company time was eight times that spent by the community educational setup and this study was done six to eight years ago! They were not including the education that goes on in the armed forces or education on the surface, which is considerable. In some countries the armed services have almost a monopoly on the higher educational process, engineering, medicine, etc. In Brazil, most of the higher education goes on in the armed forces . . . so if you want a higher education you go into the army, or navy, or air force. Even in the English-speaking countries the armed forces academies are serious educational centers. The Duke of Edinburgh had his education in the Navy, remember. In backward countries the army has crash-program education, speeded up. Most of it is war technology and related to technology, we do not fool around with the other stuff. There is no use fighting with weaponry that isn't as late as you can make it. But as far as I am concerned the older the weapons the better.

Harvey Wheeler of the Center for the Study of Democratic Institutions discusses a weird aspect of this. He says that a backward country like Vietnam can equalize its technological disadvantages with the United States by being ready to die. If the people are ready to die they can overcome the discrepancies technologically. This is, of course, the discovery of democracy. Every citizen is a guerrilla fighter, using as his target—power. Wherever there is power in the community he uses that as his target. The democratic guerrilla fighter gets his own education under battle conditions.

Socialization is having a great impact on adolescents today. It is difficult to get the kids together any more—for meals, for vacations, for anything. This is all part of the decentralization process, it is not centralization at all. Kids have everything planned out; they make their plans way in advance today; they know what they will be doing months ahead of time. This is all part of the electronic field decentralization and the Destination Syndrome—goals disappear, goals are destroyed.

Q. What effect does this have on the dropout?

Dropoutism is normal. It is also an executive trait today. There is just as much dropoutism in the top executive world, at the present time, as there is in education. Industry is taking on a maintenance role today. A lot of industries including the older and more mechanical ones, are taking more and more the character of a service industry. Where they used to just package up hardware and ship it around, now that hardware requires more and more service. When they set up computers today a man goes with them, like holding its hand, sets it up, puts it to work for the client.

Q. *Would you explain the term information environment?*

The information environment, the total environment, renders back the image of the hunter. What has come back into the world today is the hunter, which we call research or discovery. The whole enterprise educationally increasingly takes on the characteristic of the hunter. When the whole environment becomes information, you live information overload and the only strategy under those conditions is myth. Mythic structuring of situations becomes natural under information overload. You can't cope with it in classification terms, so you build myths. We now live mythically; we can't think mythically but we live mythically. This is because of electronic speed. Myth is highly speeded up information and experience, as in dreams—where you begin to move at the speed of your own nervous system; you inevitably come up with mythic structure. You do not have classified data in dream life, you have myth—multilayered, rich, fast-moving data. It is collage, transparency, etc.

Q. *What does this do to poetry and literature?*

Oh well, the poets have done their best to create mythic and depth materials and visions even in spite of industrial man; they have tried to cope with it. The role of art has always been to train perceptions of the world you live in, not of some other world. So, the older poets looked at that way are still relevant, they are attempts to make people see what is going on—painters and musicians, likewise. They are still valid.

Q. *Will the one-art skill disappear?*

Well, we have a very poetic advertisement down on Dundas Street here in Toronto. There is a sign on a junkyard that reads: "Help beautify junkyards, throw something lovely away today." It is overlayered. The moment you begin to compress even in headlines, you are heading toward poetry. Newspaper headlines tend to be very poetic, the more condensed, the more compressed they are, the more poetic. Remember the old one about "Sticks nix hick's pix"? The rejection by the rural population of the Western movie was headlined this way in *Variety*—and that is overlay!

Q. *How about the old staid newspapers, though?*

Oh, they run advertisements loaded with poetry; all of them do. Ads are sharp for that. The Bayeux tapestry is very much like modern advertising for liquors or anything. Speaking about overlay reading, *Finnegans Wake* is just like LSD. You are taking a real fast trip through many levels of consciousness. Enthusiasts for LSD seem to report a sort of superhuman ecstasy, joy—well, after all, reading *Finnegan* is fun, you just laugh your head off. It can be very funny!

Q. Is there a conclusion we can make?

Well, this brings us back to the Destination Syndrome, psychic space. Education must be done in the total field. The real work of education is growing up. Royalty only has to grow up, and they use all the available knowledge to do it. We are all in the position of royalty today, we are all growing up—that is total. Growing up as work is what the hunter does. The whole environment is involved, we sense everything. There is no childhood anymore, no one is physically inferior anymore. The prowess of the child in language is amazing; he learns a great deal in two years, then he begins to specialize.

We will be forced back into total environment. We are using crash-programming in language, brainstorming in industry, all our senses are in use at once. We will have to develop other procedures to do this in education.

Marshall McLuhan Massages the Medium

I have a friend in Toronto by the name of Leonard Frizer, who is head of the information service at the municipal education center in Toronto. He was describing to me some of the marvels of retrievable and computerized services offered to the school kids of Toronto.

Elementary school children, he said, can take any problem that they're working on to the center and get an okay on it from the school librarian. Then the order is sent along to the electronic center, and a bibliography and body of prepared materials on that particular problem for that particular student are instantly prepared by computer and Xerox and shipped to the student. This wedding of two environments, of computer and Xerox, creates quite a potent form of publication. Frizer said to me: "You know, it couldn't have happened anywhere except in a backward country."

Frizer's a New Yorker who couldn't dream of getting this sort of thing set up there because there are too many smart people who are already sufficiently advanced in the old technology to make the new technology inaccessible.

Meditate on that if you like.

Backview Is Not for Driving

Don't try to drive by means of the backview of the rearview mirror. This is a universal human tendency. I have another friend who is fond of pointing out that the future of the future is the present. All that can ever happen in the near or even quite remote future is already here now, happening, completely invisible.

The present is always invisible. We only see the past—the immediate past—but this habit of looking in rearview mirrors seems to be built on the human constitution, seems to have something to do with being born, because the moment we are born, we begin to look back where we came from as a much more desirable environment. Plato had noticed this peculiar human habit of always learning by going from the familiar to the unfamiliar. He thought it must point to a fact that we were really recalling something we had known in a previous existence, and that was how we learned—by remembering something we had already known. This is a not too satisfactory theory of knowledge, but many educators have settled for the idea that we learn by going from the familiar to the unfamiliar.

Even granting this, there is the peculiar fact that whenever we encounter the unfamiliar, we instantly translate it into the familiar and thereby never see the unfamiliar.

People never see their environments. They never know them. They always know the preceding one. This stands out loud and clear.

Kids are not the least bit impressed by our mass media. They regard them as strictly amusing, usable ploys. This is their environment—they grew up with these things as their normal human environment, and they feel at home with it. They have no intention of being suppressed or brainwashed by it. They are just going to have fun.

Advantages of Being Backward

Backward countries do have an advantage. They can leapfrog out of say the 10th century b.c. into the 20th century without any intervening processing. This happened in the U.S. in the 18th century. It was able to use the latest European technology without any impediments or inhibitions from the old feudal system and so forth. No restraints. No difficulties. The United States was able to institute a program of literacy and of publication without any restraints from the old feudal regime.

This was what fascinated de Tocqueville with the United States. He saw the latest European technologies being used in an environment where there were no objections. And this happened in another strange way on the West Coast. The American West Coast—California, and so forth—never had a 19th century. It leapfrogged out of the 18th into the 20th century.

You couldn't have Hollywood in Chicago, or New York, or any other part of the country. It had to be in an area that had been untouched by the 19th century with all of its rigorous bureaucratic methods of organization of energy. The 19th century, and especially the middle part of it, was the great period of institutionalizing and bureaucratizing human knowledge and human organizational energies.

Countries that missed that 19th century period remained flexible and adaptable, and innovational in tone and pattern. If you want to initiate advanced and revolutionary programs, try them on the West Coast.

Pavlov's Dogs and Stimuli

I was reading a book recently in which the author, Irwin Strauss, was explaining that Pavlov, the Russian psychologist, had not found it possible to condition his subjects—dogs—by stimuli. He discovered that unless they were in a carefully prepared environment, the stimuli had no effect. Pavlov conditioned his dogs by environmental means, not stimuli. This is a basic fact that has been overlooked by North American psychologists for whom the stimulus is all-important and the environment is usually ignored.

Pavlov totally controlled temperature and sound conditions—the environments. When stimuli were used, they were faint little pings—no bells, no gongs, just ping. For a Russian, of course, the total environment is an all-important and obvious thing as compared with the little fragmentary stimuli, or stimulus.

To us, the environment is not nearly so recognizable or considerable as its is to a Russian. Brainwashing is something that all environments do to us and the Russians deliberately use as teaching machines.

One of the things that is going to happen in the immediate future for us is the deliberate programing of environments instead of curriculums, the deliberate programming of environments as teaching machines, infallible teaching machines.

We Live in Bonanza-Land

In England, with the coming of industrialism, the old agrarian environment became idealized and the romantic movement resulted. When this happened, people began to ask: "Why didn't our ancestors have a more appreciative outlook on the beautiful natural world in which they lived?"

The answer is quite simple. They didn't have industrialism. Whenever people encounter a new environment, they rebuild the old one. This happened with electricity when the electric forms went around the old mechanical forms; a new awareness occurred, which we now associate with abstract art, nonrepresentational objective abstract art created by the electric circuit going around mechanical technology.

But there is a far more exciting thing happening in that department right now. As satellites and man-made environments go around the planet, the planet becomes an art form. It will undergo a complete transformation into the image of a work of art—Williamsburg style.

In the next few decades, we will lavish countless trillions of dollars upon this planet by way of rebuilding it and reshaping it and combining it and cherishing it in the forms that it once enjoyed long before human encounter.

This factor you can count on, though, as a basic operational form: Whenever a new technology creates, as it always does, a new environment, it goes around the old one and turns the old one into a work of art. Witness the late show.

Old sounds, old movies now become valued works of art. When they were environments, they were trash. Now that they are old-environments, they are cherished.

The Greeks did this for their own immediate past when the new environment of literacy was formed. The Romans did it for the Greeks. The Middle Ages did it for the Romans, the Renaissance did it for the Middle Ages. Every period forms a Bonanza-like image of the preceding period. Modern suburbia does not live in suburbia. It lives in Bonanza-land.

J. A. BATTLE

Education for the World
of 1984 and 2000

Education is defined in the *Dictionary of Education* (Carter V. Good, editor) both as "the art of making available to each generation the organized knowledge of the past" and "the aggregate of all the processes by means of which a person develops abilities, attitudes, and other forms of positive value in the society in which he lives." If the world in which today's students will be living as adults is as changed from the world of today as predicted by our experts in science and technology, then following the first definition of education could create serious consequences for students who will be adults in the world of 1984 and 2000.

If teachers today are able to teach only about what has happened in the past then education is not going to be able to prepare the young today to live in the world of 1984, much less 2000. At first, it may seem that teachers may be facing a hopeless dilemma in striving to teach their students to cope with an unknown future, but it is not at all hopeless if teachers can learn how to teach their pupils to think. Through thought man can not only make some sound predictions of what the future is to bring but he can cope with the new. What is needed most today in education is for teachers to so teach that the young will learn how to discover unknown methods of solving unknown problems. The young must be taught how to think when the method to use is not now known and the problem to be solved has not even been formulated. This is not a hopeless dilemma for those who believe that with thought almost nothing bad is inevitable and almost nothing good is impossible.

A prominent linguist has suggested recently that students today not study a foreign language but rather study *how* to learn *any* language. He says that one seldom knows until he completes school and college what language he will need and therefore the time could be better spent studying the principles of language. While I believe that students should anticipate with some degree of accuracy what languages they will need, this concept has in it a germ of an idea that we could use as teachers of students who will be adults in 1984 and 2000.

The real security for these children rests on their ability to think. Teachers who try to get them to realize this, instead of having them spend precious time memorizing the axioms that may have served the past, are striving for the more adequate future security for them. Possibly some teachers do not adopt this strategy because they are backing up into the future. They may not have developed their own intellectual capacity to see beyond what seems to be obvious, the realities of yesterday and today. But if they judge the future only in terms of the past and present they are sure to go wrong. One of the greatest mistakes teachers and other adults make today is believing that children have only a small capacity for thinking. Such a belief keeps the child from fully developing his mental capacities.

R. Buckminster Fuller, designer of the geodesic dome, is often called a genius. In an article written for the *Saturday Review*, adapted from a paper he contributed to the 50th anniversary book of the Harvard class of 1917, he wrote, "I am convinced that neither I nor any other human, past or present, was or is a genius. I am convinced that what I have, every physically normal child also has at birth. We could, of course, hypothesize that all babies are born geniuses and get swiftly degeniused. Unfavorable circumstances, shortsightedness, frayed nervous systems, and ignorantly articulated love and fear of elders tend to shut off many of the child's brain capability valves. I was lucky in avoiding too many disconnects." It is the responsibility of teachers today to find for their students connections rather than disconnections with the world they will be living in as adults.

As teachers today we need most to learn how to teach our students to succeed in a world that is unknown and may never be known by us. In other words, we need the capacity to teach what we do not know. We can begin by showing less concern for disseminating knowledge and a great concern for instructing our students so that they can direct their own lives through thought.

It is simple, comparatively speaking, to teach students how to follow a well-worn path, but it is the most difficult of tasks to teach them how to reach a destination to which there are few if any paths and, more difficult still, when the destination itself is not even known. But as teachers, if we will accept the challenge of helping the children to resolve the problems of the future when we do not know what their future will be like, our present tasks will not only be the most exciting of all possible tasks but they will be the most meaningful and important tasks of the world of today.

Chancellor JOHN GERSON, University of Paris
(1363 to 1429)

Love and Teaching

But where there is no love, what good in instruction, as one neither likes to listen to it nor properly believes in the words heard, nor follows the commandments! Therefore it is best to forego all false dignity and to become a child among children. Yet all sins have to be avoided, and all signs of impure love have to be held at bay. Also, it must be added, that our nature is inclined to resist, as Seneca proves. Our nature prefers guidance to force. Especially gifted people have the further characteristic— as the dumb creatures, the wild animals, and the birds teach us—that they are won and influenced by flattery rather than by words of threat. Why, after all, should extremely shy children hide their sins from one whom they neither hate nor fear? One who in addition had convinced them that he is benevolent, loyal, and friendly? But he will not be able to convince them unless he smiles kindly at the laughing ones, encourages those who play, praises their progress in learning, and when remonstrating, avoids all that is bitter or insulting. Then the children will feel he does not hate, but loves like a brother.

J. A. BATTLE

Don't Fall in Love with a Tool

H. Allen Smith claims that a second-grade teacher in Milwaukee greeted her children at the beginning of a new term with an assignment to write a composition on "something important you learned during your vacation." Among the essays turned in, he says was the following:

Don't Get Perconel with a Chicken

by ELOISE COLEMAN

On my vacation I visited with my gran parents in Iowa and my gran father learned me dont get perconel with a chicken. My gran father has a few chickens and one was a chicken I got perconel with and gave the name Gene Autry. One day my gran mother deside to have stood chicken for dinner and says Orf and you go out and kill a hen meening my gran father. I went with him and low and behole he took a pole with a wire on the end and reeched in the pen and got Gene Autry by the leg and pulled him out and before I cood say a werd he rung his neck wich pulls off his hed and he flops around on the grond back and forth without no hed on and I cryed. He was a brown one. Then he scalted him in hot water and picket the feathers of and saw me crying and says dont ever get perconel with a chicken. When we are at the dinner table he says it again so I ate some, a drumb stick. I dident say anything but it was like eating my own rellatives. So dont get perconel with a chicken, also a cow if you are going to eat it later on. Also a caff.*

Reading this fine essay reminded me of a conversation that I heard recently. It was on a Saturday morning as I was mowing my grass when I should have been playing tennis. There were several youngsters out in nearby Lake Carroll doing what they should have been doing on Saturday—swimming, frolicking, and talking. I heard one of the youngsters holler out, "Don't drowndun me, I like living too good!" I thought immediately that probably the boy's English teacher would rather he drown than use such grammar, although he had made his point very clear. I just hoped he had a teacher of some subject or a parent who would

* From *Don't Get Perconel with a Chicken*, copyright © 1957, 1959 by H. Allen Smith, p. 78. With permission of Little, Brown & Company.

give him a high mark for liking living so much. Of course he should improve his grammar, but I would pray that in doing so the boy does not become so prim and "refined" that he loses his zest for life—gaining such zest being a purpose for teaching English anyway. Which brings us to our third illustration of the point that I hope I am going to make later.

The late Charles F. Kettering, the inventor of the automobile self-starter, once made a friendly wager that he could drive from his home near Dayton, Ohio, to Detroit in an hour and a half less than the usually accepted driving time without breaking the speed limit. When he proved he could do this, by driving on some roads that were not used by most of the travelers between the two cities, he was told by the person with whom he made the little wager, "Oh, but you didn't do it fairly. You didn't drive on U.S. Highway 25." Kettering said that was the trouble with the thinking of most persons. They do not start with the problem in looking for solutions but with preconceptions. They want to squeeze all life into a groove.

Some persons in academic circles have been accused of worshipping their preconceptions so much that they are seldom able to find true conceptions. Those to whom this accusation applies probably do not see their favorite subject matter or method of teaching as being simply an instrument for learning to live a finer life. Some of those who did not recognize their academic idol as only a tool for learning took part a few years ago in the "great debate" on subject matter versus method. In this debate one side claimed that it was for teaching subject matter and the other side stated that it was for teaching people. Both sides probably should have said that they were for teaching subject matter to people or using subject matter to teach people.

In teaching one cannot make a choice between subject matter or method, but one has to make a choice as to whether either is to be used as a tool or a ritual. While the issue in the "great debate" was sometimes rightly defined on the basis of the needed quantity and the quality of substantive and procedural knowledge for excellent instruction, this question is not the source of the significant ideological difference among teachers. The important issue is whether the teaching specialties are regarded as an end in themselves or as one area of knowledge to be utilized in an exploratory spirit. But the debators were so intense about eliminating the specialties of the other side and were so absorbed in their own specialities, or self-interest, that they hardly recognized this as an issue.

The person who believes it violates the sacredness of his speciality to use it as an instrument for learning may be like the old farmer, Harold Benjamin told the writer about, who took his son to matriculate at the University of Minnesota. The farmer told the dean that he wanted his boy to study Greek because of what he considered the inherent virtues in the subject, which he stated as follows: "First, it's hard, second, my boy won't like it and finally, it's the kind of subject that won't do him no good."

While a teacher should "get personal" with both his subject and method, sometimes almost to the point of loving them, he cannot, if he wants his pupils to become educated, make either form of knowledge an object of worship. Actually one who has learned to love learning does not worship a tool for learning, because it may become obsolete and be a hindrance to improving his learning.

To be used effectively knowledge, whether substantive or procedural, cannot be thought of as coming from an oracle. Instead it must be utilized as a means for seeking truth. Such an approach makes it possible for the learner's life to be brightened, his fancy caught, and his soul stirred.

ROBERT L. SHANNON

Problems to Ponder

You will encounter some amazing circumstances in teaching. It will be interesting to see how you stand the test, how you respond to certain instances, and how well you are able to apply what you know about education in our society and what you know about how people learn as you find solutions to some perplexing problems. You are about to examine some actual experiences of teachers who were in situations quite similar to those in which you will soon find yourself. What would you do in each of these situations? What action would you take? Can you justify your ideas on the basis of what is fundamental in the philosophy of education in our society? Are your solutions fulfilling those principles of learning that have been proved valid? What suggestions will you have for putting your proposals into operation in each of these circumstances?

Guidance for Jack

"No sir, no sir, Mr. King, I ain't got them pencils. I don't know nothing about how them pencils got out of the store." Presenting a face of complete innocence, Jack continued to insist that he had no knowledge of some stolen pencils that were missing from the neighborhood grocery store.

Mr. King, the junior high school principal, again faced seventh-grade Jack with a problem. "Jack, there is no need in your denying it any further. The store owner saw you take the pencils, watched you put them in your pocket, and permitted you to leave the store so that we could track you down. Now we know that you stole those pencils, and you have been stealing all along. Now we expect you to acknowledge this theft and begin to make things right."

"I ain't got them pencils, Mr. King. I just ain't got them. I don't know nothing about them pencils."

Continuing the exchange of accusation followed by denial for another forty minutes, Mr. King elected to prove his point. "Okay, Jack, come with me."

At this point Jack was led down the hallway, through the school, into the gymnasium, and into a boys' rest room where some privacy was as-

111

sured. "Jack, I'll give you one last opportunity. You stole those pencils. I know it; you know it. Now I'm asking you to give them to me and tell me about the entire incident. This is your last opportunity."

Once again jack repeated his innocence. "All right, Jack. This is your decision. Now you are to begin stripping. Take off each item of clothing and hand it to me as you remove each item, and I'll want to search it myself."

Completely perplexed, Jack removed his shirt, his undershirt, his trousers, his shoes, his socks, handing each item to Mr. King for an examination. Having made this thorough examination, Jack was standing in his shorts waiting for Mr. King to return his clothing. "No, now, Jack, now the shorts, now the shorts."

"But, Mr. King, surely I couldn't put the pencils in my shorts."

"Hand me your shorts. I insist on examining those, too."

At this, Jack removed his underwear, handing it to Mr. King in a final expression of complete defeat. Clipped inside the fly of Jack's shorts were three gleaming, new pencils. Mr. King had found the pencils and had proved Jack guilty of the crime. The final step was to call the appropriate juvenile authorities, who took Jack to court and ultimately placed him on probation for a period of time. Jack had stolen the pencils. Mr. King had been successful in proving his guilt.

What response do you have to the manner in which this problem was handled? Can you defend the principal's position? If you are in opposition to the principal's handling of this situation, what suggestions do you have and how will you defend your action?

A Teacher Seeks Silence

The bell rings, indicating time for recess. The youngsters in your third-grade room anxiously put their books away and prepare for the fifteen minutes on the playground. Busily conversing with some of the students, you wander from the room and into the hall, for banging of lockers and giggling of children bring quick relief from the busy activity of the previous hour. Passing by Miss Franklin's room with your happy crowd, your eyes suddenly are confronted with a sight you cannot believe. Standing in the doorway of Miss Franklin's room is Jimmy—the bubbling, excitable Jimmy who can never be quiet, who always has something to say, who is bursting with enthusiasm whenever you have met. But this Jimmy is silent—an enforced silence that has no possibility of being broken. Jimmy's mouth is taped shut. Covering his mouth and much of his face you see a mask of adhesive tape. You immediately inquire as to what has happened. Jimmy is silent and quickly moves away.

When you reach the playground other children in Jimmy's room come to tell you what has happened. How can you ethically respond to what you hear? "Miss Franklin couldn't stand Jimmy's talking any more," is the excited report by Janie. "So, she taped his mouth shut, and he has to leave it on there all day." You suggest a game for the girls, and they go on their way, but the problem remains with you.

Recess, the remainder of the morning, and lunch in the afternoon pass as usual. However, Jimmy is the only thing that is on your mind. As school is dismissed for the day, you anxiously wait in the hallway to watch Miss Franklin's room leave for home. As Jimmy walks by the door, Miss Franklin gives him a look of complete disgust, removes the tape from his face, and sends him on his way without a word.

When you arrive for school the next morning, you drop into Miss Franklin's room to borrow some chalk. Five minutes before school starts, Jimmy already has the same tape over his face. What will you do? During this day and the next Jimmy is covered with exactly the same adhesive tape mask that provides enforced silence. On the fourth day Jimmy is not required to wear the tape on his mouth, and he is silent.

You are the teacher across the hall. What will you do? How will you respond? What is your ethical obligation?

A Decision for the Cafeteria

Astonishing interest was shown in the Monday morning bulletin. Your excited teaching companion in the room down the hall hustles through the doorway with her bulletin in hand. "What do you think of that? What do you think of that?" She sputters, confident that she has the finest news item of the week. As curious as the next, you begin to examine your daily bulletin. Drab, purple printing of the inevitable ditto machine greets your eyes as you scan down the list of collections for the week, committee obligations, PTA announcements, library fines, articles in the lost and found, and then the administrative edict. This can't be! It's surely an exaggeration. I couldn't do that. Let's just wait and see what happens. Read through. What does it say? Your eyes digest the words of the administrative decision. In the past few weeks talking in the lunchroom has become excessive. Something must be done to correct this problem. Children are making far too much noise as they eat their lunch. Therefore, beginning today and until further notice there will be absolutely no talking in the lunchroom during the lunch periods. Students will enter the lunchroom, pick up their trays, go to the nearest table or to the table assigned, be seated, eat their lunch, and promptly leave the cafeteria without talking. That is what you read, but you cannot believe it. Your fellow teacher assures you that this is what will occur, but you remain a skeptic and feel that the noon hour will be carried on as usual.

When it is time for your room to go to the lunchroom, you find that what might be a fable is fact. Absolute silence prevails. To be certain that his announcement is carried out to the letter, the principal is standing guard in the lunchroom fulfilling an effective police role.

What will you do? How will you approach this problem? How will you support your action?

The Principal Solves a Problem

You are a junior high school teacher working with the abundant problems faced by persons in early adolescence. As in many schools, your program is unsuccessful in fulfilling the needs of all students. A special problem appears to be present with a group of seventh-grade boys who are apparently dissatisfied with their personal attainments and with their total school experience. In the boys' rest room a rash of writing on the walls has appeared. The scribblings take the form of obscene words and pictures scrawled hurriedly and crudely. Sensitive to the problem you and another teacher begin the long-term problem of getting to the basis of this psychological difficulty. The task is time consuming, painstaking, providing little progress. You and your fellow teacher feel that you are on your way to identifying the boys who are having the difficulty and are beginning to work with them to understand what is provoking their need to write on the wall.

Impatient with your progress, the principal takes the situation in hand, goes into the room, and forces a confession out of the culprits. Having identified the boys responsible for this behavior, he removes them from class, acquires the necessary buckets, soap, and brushes, and marches them down to the rest room. The next move is to demand that they scrub down the walls with soap and water while he triumphantly observes their compelled interest in cleanliness. Many hours are required to clean up the rest room, but the principal patiently perseveres while the boys begrudgingly fulfill their assigned task. Finally, the obscenities are removed, and the rest room is immaculate. Your principal then ends the experience by saying, "There you are, boys, now let's just look at this wall together. Doesn't it look better? Aren't you proud of what you've done? Sure you are. It's a job well done. Now we expect you to keep the rest room this way and for this problem not to appear again. Now you may go back to your rooms." Having solved the problem efficiently and effectively, the principal finishes out the day and goes home with immense satisfaction—another problem has been remedied.

Before school begins the next day one of your students comes to you reluctantly but with a message concerning the rest room. You immediately go to the rest room and find scribbled on the walls in immense letters this message: "To hell with the principal." Obviously, the problem was only intensified by the principal's actions. What will you do?

What to Do with Smokers?

You are a high school teacher. The girls in the school where you teach have discovered that smoking is a stylish and satisfying pastime. School rules, however, prohibit smoking on the school grounds and in the school buildings. In typical adolescent fashion, this intensifies the girls' interest in smoking and encourages them to devise many schemes for smoking on the school grounds and in the schoolrooms. The girls have developed a successful code of behavior that apparently is impossible to defeat.

The smell of your favorite brand floats through the window, and you are immediately certain that someone is smoking in the rest room. Certain to apprehend the offenders, you hurry to the rest room door only to be given a friendly greeting by Mary Ann, one of the dependable young ladies, who says, "Good morning." As you enter the smoke-filled rest room, you are greeted by the sound of flushing toilets. But no one can be detected smoking. Obviously, the friendly greeting served a dual purpose as a signal and hello. You know the girls are violating school rules, but you are unable to find any evidence to that effect. What will you do? Why?

"As educators, we have moved easily and effectively in the world of ideas. We have, I think, now to learn the more difficult art of moving easily and effectively among people."

By What Means Do We Teach?

In order to attain the objectives of education for our society certain decisions are made concerning what will be studied in schools. Sometimes the curriculum is called the environment in which education takes place. Another definition restricts curriculum to a group of selected subjects taught in the school. Perhaps neither of these definitions is quite right. You will want to formulate a definition of curriculum that is appropriate to use as a basis for selecting what the schools will teach in order to accomplish their purposes.

As you read, evaluate these curriculum ideas in relation to the proper aims of education in our society.

What Is Your Judgment?

Should everyone be taught the fundamentals? What are they? Are they the same for all people?

Schools should eliminate the frills. What is a frill?

Taking only two years of a foreign language is considered a waste of time. What do you think?

What is counseling?

Should vocational counseling be a part of the high school guidance program? If so, what should this be like?

What is study? Does teaching have anything to do with study?

Can television teach? If so, what are important qualities of a program if it is to teach?

Can one learn from a teaching machine?

HAROLD BENJAMIN

The Riding, Shooting, Truth-Speaking Curriculum

The ancient Persians, according to Herodotus, had a simple curriculum; they taught their boys to ride, to shoot, and to speak the truth. These essentials of their schooling were presumably derived from what they thought were the major needs of their society. The horse was their chief instrument of transport. The bow was their primary weapon. The sanctity of their word was the heart of their ethics. To the extent that excellence in these matters could be developed by instruction, the main elements of their education were clearly designated for them.

When the Persians had decided on the educational experiences that would make their children good members of the family, the clan, the tribe, and the nation, they had answered the first basic question confronting every people who would develop a formal educational system. How shall we teach these children to be better members of our society?

As soon as the Persians or anyone else attempts to answer the first question adequately, however, they run into the task of looking at the total pattern of the child's learning outside school. What does and what should this boy learn in the home, the market place, the temple, or anywhere else? What can and what should be taught to him in the school?

Most pressing of all reasons for this examination of the entire set of influences affecting the child's behavior has always been the concern of every group for the learning of what it considered to be necessary moral and spiritual values. What education will make this child good for himself and his people?

The next curricular concern of a people seeking to educate their children was the integration of the various parts of the learning experience. Did expert horsemanship need to be correlated with marksmanship? Was straight shooting connected in any way with straight talking and thinking?

The final question concerning a curriculum is the extent to which it is going to be given to all or only to selected learners. In ancient Persia were the sons of horseless men to be given instruction in equitation? Were girls to be taught to use the bow? Were all children to be brought up to the same standard of truth?

A. S. NEILL

School Subjects as the Natural Enemy of the Child

The Teacher and the School Subject

I have already suggested that the school subject is one of the means used by the State to prevent the child from being educated. It is a safety valve. The only dangerous subject is History, and the textbooks are so written that they are almost dangerproof. Fortunately the State cannot eliminate the teacher's adding his own version to that of the approved book unless it is a State of the totalitarian type with a terror behind its commands.

The other subjects are only useless and sidetracking. This is especially true of the secondary school in which boys learn the Theory of Quadratics before they go out to deliver newspapers or beef. They learn French which they are compelled by life to forget when they leave school, compelled because they can never go to France, and having learned mostly the grammar, can never read a French book with ease or pleasure. The little Chemistry and Physics they acquire cannot possibly be kept up after school is left, for no clerk, no shopkeeper, no tradesman has the apparatus or facility for going on with the subject. We rightly thunder against dead end occupations, for nearly every subject is a dead end one.

The elementary school is less dangerous than the secondary school. Its ambition is less: it is more or less content with the Three R's, that is, the tools necessary for further education. The teacher is not a specialist in one subject, and is able to avoid the narrowness that the subject specialist is almost bound to acquire. True the elementary school has its own dead ends of the long division, multiplication of vulgar and decimal fractions variety, yet in the main the elementary teacher does good work and too often gets the minimum of appreciation for it. He has the chance, if he can take it, to give children up to fourteen a liberal education, in spite of the Education Code. I think of some of the rural schools I knew in

A. S. Neill, *The Problem Teacher*, London, Jenkins Publishing Company, copyright 1944, pp. 40–53. Reprinted by permission of Collins-Knowlton-Wing, Inc.

121

Scotland long ago. The village teacher often did give his pupils a good education for that time. This was largely due to the fact that, having four to six classes to attend to, he had to leave the children to themselves for long periods, but it was also due to the ability of the teacher to teach in an interesting way.

I can never take the evergreen controversy about the school-leaving age seriously. I see no point in keeping children at school as schools are today. If a boy leaves a secondary school at seventeen instead of fifteen he will only have a larger smattering of dead end subjects to dump before he begins his life work. Under a sensible and just civilization a boy would probably be allowed to remain at school 'til he was nineteen, but the school would be adapted to his psychological needs, and the subjects would be very minor affairs in it.

Both elementary and secondary schools fail to be educative because they only provide for the intellect and the memory. Education should be creative all the time, but every schoolmaster knows that his work is almost without creation. Only when creation is recognized as the only dynamic factor in education will our schools be real places of education. So long as learning poetry is preferred to writing verse: so long as vulgar fractions on a blackboard are of more moment than fractions used creatively in making something in wood or metal, our schools are failing to educate.

Most teachers have a more or less vague feeling that their work is pouring water down a drain. In a way the unconscious teacher who thinks that his little subject is a big subject is the lucky one. The really tragic teacher is he who feels keenly that he is giving his best to an unworthy cause, fighting a battle under a flag that he does not honour. Other professions are envious of the teacher's short hours and long holidays. The teacher needs them more than the children do: his work is psychically much more exhausting than that of a lawyer or doctor, not only because he has to regress to the level of the child all the time, but also because he has a job that never finishes, a job in which he never can see the end. The barrister after a trial can say with a sigh of relief: Something attempted, something done: the doctor can say it after the recovery . . . or the funeral. The teacher can never say it. His is a voice crying in the wilderness, and he never knows how much the young ears have taken in. He is in very much the same position as the man who screws a certain nut on a car that travels along the belt: he never sees the completed car. The simile suggests that about the only thing a teacher has to do is to screw on one nut and leave the car to be completed by experience. Our schools are as much mass production factories as the Ford or Morris works.

I don't want to carry the comparison too far. Ford knows what kind of a car he wants, but no teacher knows or should know what kind of a man or woman he should produce from his factory. It is right that the teacher should never see the end of his work. If, however, he had some confidence in the beginning of his work, if he felt that he was on the right lines, he would do more valuable work and would enjoy it more. That is why I manage to have a staff in Summerhill. The teachers know that they are coming to a salary that is wretched compared with what they could earn in a State school, yet they prefer to do this because they know that they can work optimistically in their own way, content in the belief that freedom will turn out a Rolls Royce that has not been made by mass production. (This, of course, is just swank on my part, for Summerhill has produced one or two T Fords as well as some Rolls Royces.)

It is the inability to see the end of his work that makes it so incumbent on a teacher to be politically minded, that is to look beyond and ahead. His subject may be his bread and butter, but he should look for his cake outside the school. If he doesn't he will stagnate and become what so many are, a mechanical drudge with his eye on the clock.

Now I am being skittish, yet I cannot see what attitude one can take up other than a humorous one. The whole subject racket is a joke, only the specialists cannot see it, and the children dare not see it. When Smith Minor is fifty how much will it matter to him or any one else what opinion his English teacher gave of him when he was twelve? Negatively it may matter a lot, for the millions of school reports that have been issued have helped to lower the self-confidence of millions of children: have given unnecessary fears to millions of children. This is known to all of you who carried home the damning Report to a father you knew would be irate.

But it isn't the Report that is the culprit: the evil lies in the teachers' attitude to the subject. If Reports are to be retained I propose that they should be written by the children themselves, about themselves with an appendix about each teacher. Such a Report might run something like this:

"I hate Maths and the Maths Mistress is a beast. I like English because Mr. Brown lets us write gangster stories or anything we like. My history is pretty bloody, but Miss Green is so dreadfully dull with her tiresome talk about Roman Civilization. Handwork is O.K. in a way, but we aren't allowed to make what we want to. Who wants to make a pen tray? I want to make guns and aeroplanes. I loathe drawing since Miss X came because she keeps breathing down the back of my neck all the time. Worse still she eats garlic."

What an excellent thing it would be for schools if the children were allowed to write Reports of their own! How spring-cleaning! How disastrous to century-old cobwebs! How exhilarating to subject specialists! How humanizing such Reports would be! Alas, most of the Reports would be lies: even if they could be published in a School Magazine anonymously, each critical child would fear that anonymity would fail to protect from staff vengeance. This subject leads on to the next chapter, The Teacher and Psychology.

The Teacher and Psychology

In the medical profession the students are taught much more about disease than about health. I do not know how it is now but in past years the medical course did not include the subject of diet. The big London hospitals still feed their convalescent patients on white bread. The interest in and the knowledge of diet came from outside the profession, and long before science had discovered Vitamin C, lay practitioners were feeding their patients on lettuce and lemons and oranges. It is seldom that one comes across a medical practitioner who attempts to go to the root of a disease. If I have a skin disease the average doctor will treat the skin without inquiring what is wrong with my living conditions that an outbreak of pimples should take place. He has been taught to treat symptoms, and that is why so many patients have fled to the lay Nature Cure man, for he, at least, puts the symptom in a second place and tries to build up the general health. He has successes because his method is fundamental.

The training of the teacher has similar limitations to those of the medical training. We might compare it to the training that makes a doctor a specialist in say—Ear, Nose and Throat. We should be reluctant to call in such a specialist to an appendix case.

The hospitals give a man training in diagnosis and general treatment and he goes out to treat bodies that medical science knows very little about. So the universities and training colleges equip a young teacher to go out and deal with human personalities that he knows little about. Because I take a B.A. in Classics at Oxford I am automatically supposed to be able to teach Latin and Greek. If I spend two years at a training college I am qualified to guide and control a group of children, even although my training has taught me nothing whatever about the nature of a child.

The teacher's chief concern should be the psychology of the child, and all school subjects should be relegated to an inferior place. The issue is evaded by the adoption of the easiest method—that of discipline. Keep the class in order so that you can hand your stuff over the footlights. Obviously if an actor wants to put his stuff across the footlights he has to make it such that his audience will discipline themselves in order to hear it. The method of the theatre should be the only one applicable to the school: the well-graced actor would command interest, while the actor whose prattle was merely tedious would find himself declaiming to empty benches.

Discipline is the substitute for knowledge of children. True enough it is necessary so long as school is an institution that for the most part militates against child nature: so long as children are compelled to sit at desks and to learn what they have no wish to learn, school discipline will be found necessary. But although today the child is made for the school, there is reason to believe that tomorrow the school will be made for the child. The new era will come much more quickly if the teachers assist in the birth of it, and that they cannot do if they are ignorant of child nature and if they accept the old discipline as a gospel.

Today the chief law in school is: Thou shalt obey. But the chief law in life is: Thou shalt refuse to obey. The only obedience of value is the obedience a man has to his inner self. All external obediences are a curse to his growth. In its psychological component this is the conflict between Fascism and Democracy. Grant that democracy is largely a sham, that the workers in this democratic country are slaves to their capitalist masters. Grant that, but deep down in their hearts the people of Britain desire freedom from obedience, freedom to get rid of the indignity of being yes-men. The men of the International Brigade were democrats who obeyed their own leaders because their leaders had the same cause as they had. That obedience is necessary. The obedience of the school is stamped with the other kind of motive: it is the Heil, Hitler variety, the army variety. Theirs not to reason why.

Obedience should be dynamic: its purpose should be the wish of the one who obeys and at the same time the wish of the one who commands. I think of the orchestral conductor and the band. Obedience should be reciprocal: if the child obeys the teacher the teacher ought to obey the child. To the old-fashioned teacher this may sound nonsense, but I have had this reciprocity in my school for many years, and it has been a complete success. Our school laws are made by the community by majority vote, and I have to obey them just as dutifully as the child of five has. I can order a child out of my room when I don't want his presence, and he can order me out of his room for a similar reason. We both obey.

That this system could not be readily applied to a disciplined and desk school is evident. For one thing it requires not only a study of child nature: it requires an infinite faith in children, and perhaps of more moment, an infinate faith in one's own attitude to the child. It implies a

Weltanschauung that relegates knowledge to its proper place, that believes that what a child knows is much less important than what a child is. In other words it makes human behavior the chief factor in education.

Yet I wonder if teachers were trained for ten years in child psychology would they be prepared to drop their pedestal position? Many, of course, would, as many do already. Teaching is not a science: it is a special kind of art, and it may be that only the artist can teach properly. I do not mean by teaching the presentation of a lesson: I mean the art of living with children and understanding them, and being one of them. Belonging to the gang, as that great teacher Homer Lane put it. A gramophone can present a good lesson just as a soulless gramophonic teacher can never really get into vital contact with the child.

That is the question—to get in vital touch with the child. To see the school and to see life from the child's point of view. The old idea that a child has to be guided is as false and stupid as Solomon's law about the stick.

What is a child? A child is a being that is largely unconscious. Its life is in great measure spent in phantasy and its play is an expression of this life. Childhood is playhood. The child is naturally active and noisy and unaware (as the state of the furniture in my school testifies). It is primarily concerned with doing, not with thinking—phantasy thinking, yes: reality thinking, no. That comes later.

Now in the classroom the phantasy side of the child has no outlook except the dangerous one of day-dreaming instead of attending to the lesson. The active side is inhibited by the necessity of sitting still, under an ignorant teacher in sitting with arms folded. The noisy side is completely suppressed until playtime. The creative side in a desk school has the minimum of opportunity for expression.

Head work is the rule of the school. This is against the holy law of child nature. Head work belongs to a later stage, much later than we think perhaps. We apply rules to children that we would never think of applying to adults. We have no desire to convert into thinkers Charles Chaplin or Greta Garbo. Many golfing teachers admire the prowess of Henry Cotton, but not one would try to improve his game by advising him to get up the history of the Hundred Years' War. The boy at the bottom of the class may be the future golf champion of England, but we treat him as if it were taken for granted that he is to be a professor.

Think what is behind the child we see sitting at a desk. We know what his arithmetic is like, but we don't know what is behind the insincere mask that conventional discipline compels him to wear all day long. Let me guess a few of the things behind his mask. He is concerned about his origin and the lies told to him about it. He is concerned about his sex, wondering if he will die or go to hell if he touches his genitals. He is concerned with all sorts of home problems, his fear of father when father raises his voice, his jealousy of his brothers and sisters. Perhaps he has a guilty conscience because he stole something, or because he told a big lie. Maybe he thinks anxiously about death. In all likelihood he is filled with fears, trembling to walk in the dark. Then there is religion. Who is God or is there a God? Further fears because of the dangerous thought. These among a thousand other troubles and doubts.

And his teacher sees only the mask, his teacher is only interested in his work, not realizing that all the hidden hopes and fears can easily destroy the ability to concentrate on work. The frequent nervous breakdowns in school children are due to education's complete disregard for the deep traits of character. Many a new parent says to me: "The last school overworked my boy." In Norway, where I am now, the overworking is worse than it is in England, for here apparently you can't become a scavenger without passing an examination. If Norwegian children are not more neurotic than English children it must be because their wonderful open-air life of skiing and skating counteracts the stupidity of their national education.

The class teacher may reply: It isn't my job to deal with the inner life of the child. I am paid for teaching the little devil arithmetic. Yes, but whose job is it then? Suppose Tommy has phobias: suppose he has inordinate death fears or wishes: suppose he is miserably unhappy. If the teacher cannot help him who can? Not his parents, not the clergyman, not the local doctor. If he steals, your punishment will make him worse, for he is seeking love and you will give him hate. If you punish him for bullying he will retain his bullying attitude longer than he would have done because he is reinforced by the added knowledge that you are also a bully.

It is the teacher's job to be the soul doctor to the child, to every child in the classroom. This, of course, cannot be carried out if the teacher attempts to serve God and Mammon, to be the soul doctor and the sergeant-major at one and the same time. In my own work I have this difficulty. New children identify me for a long time with their former teachers, and if these teachers have been strict disciplinarians, I find that it takes me weeks and often months to get into touch with the child. Only when they feel that I am not an authority do they come to me with their soul troubles. When children come young enough, at three to seven, they never show this hate and fear of authority, but then when they come so young they seldom need much in the way of soul-doctoring.

Teachers have often said to me: "It's all very well for you. You have been at the job for years, but although I want to help kids sometimes, I simply don't know how to begin. I don't know enough about psychology."

But neither do I. I may know more than many teachers because I have concentrated on the subject for years, but if a child has night terrors I have to begin at the beginning and slowly try to find out, by what the child says, what the possible cause is. Sometimes I succeed: sometimes I fail. In the latter case the trouble often disappears mysteriously without the root having been discovered. The cure is in all likelihood due to the comfort the child finds in getting an adult to side with it and comfort it.

I really do not think a training in psychology is so necessary as a sympathetic attitude. It must be non-moral. You would have to receive with as much emotion the news that a child has murdered its grandmother, as the news that the child had got a new teddy bear. It would depend on your attitude to your own grandmother anyway.

A moral attitude judges and condemns. In a teacher such an attitude is fatal. Even if the teacher hides it with a smile or a look of indifference the child feels it, for he has so uncanny a gift of seeing behind the adult mask.

Most teachers know or should know the story of how Homer Lane cured a rebel by encouraging him to break plates and saucers. I visited Norman MacMunn's school in Tiptree Hall round about 1920. Later when I saw Lane I told him this story:

"MacMunn tried your method and it failed. His boys began to break up the classroom and Norman thought he would do what you did with your destructive lad, so he joined in and helped them to complete the destruction. Then there was hell, for the boys all began to cry."

"That was because he only acted consciously," was Lane's verdict. "The boys felt that he was swindling them and of course they wept."

There is a warning in the story. One can only help the child if one is sincere in doing it. Otherwise the child will classify the teacher with the bishops and other moral danger.

The art of teaching is the art of leaving children alone. It is a most difficult art to acquire if one is not born a believer in freedom. The natural instinct of an adult is to mix in and show the child the way. This is bad enough when the way is only the way to draw a straight line, but it is tragically wrong when the way is the way to live. It takes infinite patience not to mix in. I watched with fearful doubt a boy from the age of seven to eighteen, watched him making mistakes, watched him waste his time (apparently). He is now doing a difficult job well.

But the poor class teacher cannot wait. The mill goes on grinding and he must feed it with raw fodder. As the years go on he comes to expect more chaff than golden grains. With the best mill in the world how can any teacher get into contact with the souls of forty, fifty, perhaps sixty children? I can take a child to my little Private Lesson room, but where can an L.C.C. teacher take a boy or girl in his barrack school? I am free to tell a child that there is no harm in masturbation, but if a State teacher did so he might well lose his job. I can run a school without religion, and tell the children a story of their going to heaven and finding God a benevolent old gentleman who keeps bees, but the State teacher is never free to reject religion or to make it human.

So I am forced to return to the sad truth that until the schools are humanized the teachers cannot be human or even honest. The chains cannot fall from the ankles of the children until the slave teachers are freed from their own bondage. Perhaps when our capitalist civilization has disappeared for ever . . . but I often doubt if Socialism will retain our prison schools, because the abolition of profit does not necessarily imply the miraculous transformation of mankind from moralism to humanity.

J. A. BATTLE

"Progressive Education"—
Good or Bad?

The term *progressive education* has become a part of our American folk-lore. To most of our citizens it raises an image of domineering children among docile adults. A typical cartoon of the day depicts a man lamenting that when he was a child his father was the boss, and now that he is a father his child is the boss. Then he wonders when his turn to be boss will come. The implication of the cartoon is that the blame for the present sad state of the man's parental role is to be placed squarely on the shoulders of "progressive education."

Recently on a well-known television program there was a scene in which a house painter (actually a detective) hears a woman scream. He rushes into a bedroom where there are two women, one being in a state of hysteria. The other exclaims angrily to the pseudo painter: "Don't you know better than not to knock when you enter a lady's bedroom. You must have been brought up under progressive education."

The best-selling novel by Patrick Dennis, *Auntie Mame,* makes a tongue-in-cheek comparison of two private schools—a traditional, snob-minded New England academy, termed an "academic wilderness," and a New York City school that accents "progressive education." Neither school proves to be very educational, but the "progressive" school offers a far more interesting curriculum! It is so interesting, in fact, that is is raided by the police after which the author states: "The tabloids, caught in a lull between ax murders, become profoundly pious about all of progressive education. They ran numerous articles written by civic leaders and an outraged clergy, each of which seemed to begin with the sentence, 'Mother, what is your child being taught?'"

To be considered a good American today by many of our citizens, one has to stand firmly for motherhood and at least verbalize opposition to sin and "progressive education"—among other things. Fortunately, there is no legitimate issue about motherhood. As for sin, its wages are well

From *The Torch*, 35, no. 1 (January, 1962), 45–49.

known and plenty of students are working on both sides of the subject. On the other hand, few have taken the time to seek out the facts or the theory of "progressive education." Just the other day an outspoken college professor of political science publicly lashed out at "progressive education" for being "a cult which opposes individualism." If there ever was a nonscholarly statement, that was it. The first commandment of "progressive education" is that individual differences be recognized!

To oppose either sin or "progressive education" intelligently and constructively, one must use facts instead of folklore. Only through truth is there hope of separating good from evil and putting each of them in their manageable forms.

The Origins of Progressive Education

As a first step in evaluating "progressive education," we need to ask ourselves why it ever developed and what are its aims. One of the best sources of the answers is John Dewey, who was one of the first exponents in America of the ideas we now group under the term *progressive education*.

Out of the expanded democracy after the Civil war, free public education flourished in America. John Dewey grew to maturity during this period. He saw public education confronted with many difficult problems. The demand for public education had risen so rapidly that there were far too many would-be beneficiaries to be taught with any degree of quality with the available teachers and facilities. To take care of the vast number of pupils, the emerging public school had to put its trust in a uniform and ordered school life, not unlike a great many schools of today. Its chief stock of learning consisted of graded and classified subjects, taught on a clock-like schedule with definite years being reserved for mastering definite assorted facts and operations. Teaching was reduced to shoveling knowledge into pupils and administering massive doses of homework and examinations. The discipline, unlike that of today, was as a whole geared to the reform school. Pupils' accomplishments, such as they were, were recorded as grades, the best of which went not necessarily to those who were creative—the Woodrow Wilsons and Thomas Edisons—but to those who had camera-like minds that could reproduce and parrot the biggest array of facts. As a student of the history of education in America has said of the public school before the 20th century, "Though impregnated with high motives, it was obviously more the drill ground than the house of Solomon. Specializing in the gross, it was expected to yield a standardized product."

Dewey wanted to change this standardized system by (1) giving the pupil opportunity for self-expression and cultivation of individuality, (2) having the pupils learn through experience, (3) motivating, not by drill, but by presenting ends that make a direct, vital appeal to the pupil, (4) getting pupils concerned about the importance of the present, including schooling itself, instead of a remote future, and getting them used to the idea that life is not static, but ever changing.

Dewey contrasted the traditional educational programs of his day with his new philosophy as follows:

1. To imposition from above is opposed expression and cultivation of individuality.

2. To external discipline is opposed free activity.

3. To learning from texts and teachers is opposed learning through experience.

4. To acquisition of isolated skills and techniques by drill is opposed acquisition of them as means of attaining ends which make a direct, vital appeal.

5. To preparation for a more or less remote future is opposed making the most of the opportunities of present life.

6. To static aims and materials is opposed acquaintance with a changing world.

At the national convention of Kappa Delta Pi in 1928, Dewey summarized his position in an address on *The Sources of a Science of Education* as follows:

> The main purpose or objectives (of traditional education) is to prepare the young for future responsibilities and for success in life by means of acquisition of the organized bodies of information and prepared forms of skills which comprehended the material of instruction. Since the subject matter as well as standards of proper conduct are handed down from the past, the attitude of pupils must, upon the whole, be one of docility, receptivity, and obedience. Books, especially textbooks, are the chief representatives of the lore and wisdom of the past, while teachers are the organs through which pupils are brought into effective connection with the material. Teachers are the agents through which knowledge and skills are communicated and rules of conduct enforced.
>
> I have not made this brief summary for the purpose of criticizing the underlying philosophy. The rise of what is called new education and progressive schools is of itself a product of discontent with traditional education. In effect it is a criticism of the latter. The traditional scheme is, in essence, one of imposition from above and outside. It imposes adult standards, subject-matter, and methods upon those who are only growing slowly toward maturity. The gap is so great that the required subject-matter, and methods of learning and behaving are

foreign to the existing capacities of the young. They are beyond the reach of the experience the young learners already possess. Consequently, they must be imposed, even though good teachers will use devices of art to cover up the imposition so as to relieve it of obviously brutal features.*

Dewey believed that in his system children learned better to think and to assume responsibility because they were given choices and an opportunity for experiences. Dewey was a reformer. As a result of his efforts and those of like-minded persons, American education did, to some extent, become more dynamic, more alive, and more like America. Some of the old European patterns were either abandoned or modified. The German drill system no longer predominated, at least on the surface, although in most schools there was still not a great deal of opportunity for the pupil to act as an individual except in extra-curricular activities, which naturally became his chief interests.

In the beginning of the twentieth century all sorts of plans had been devised to loosen up the formal curriculum and give it life and vitality—projects, activities, excursions and visits, gardens, laboratories, and visual aids—anything to overcome the slavish drill on the textbook or notebook. There was little doubt that for most children the quality of learning was somewhat raised as vitality and zest were added to the learning process. In general, however, teachers talking and bored pupils only sometimes listening were still predominant in American public education. The most significant change was in the broadening of the curriculum to include the so-called vocational subjects—agriculture, industrial arts, home economics, and even driver education. Since the ordinary American has never been interested in the intellectual life and his children predominated in the democratically controlled public schools, the so-called intellectual subjects such as history, English, and mathematics were often neglected. Schooling continued to be a bore to the average pupil, but in the few truly progressive schools, in the sense John Dewey wanted them to be, vitality and zest were added to the learning process.

Schools Called "Too Soft"

In the 1940's and 1950's a new set of "reformers" came to the forefront. They charged that the schools were too soft. Their leaders were college professors who were dissatisfied with the public school preparation of their pupils. Even parents made these same charges. However, public school

* John Dewey, *The Sources of a Science of Education*, The Kappa Delta Pi Lecture Series, New York, No. 1, Liveright, 1929.

teachers often got into trouble when they stiffened the requirements. But the reformers persisted. The schools, they said, were just letting children play and not teaching them anything. One typical charge was made by a parent who said that his child had been taught in the first grade how to make ashtrays, which pleased his teacher because of their fine quality, but had not been taught how to read. So elementary schools were exhorted to return to the three R's (meaning "readin', 'ritin', and regimentation," contended the former liberals, now classified as reactionaries) and to stiffer discipline and concentration on intellectual study. The Soviet Sputnik and the Soviet educational system strengthened the critics' hand.

Many of the criticisms were overdrawn and unfair, but there was truth in some. Progressive methods had been grossly misinterpreted by many of Dewey's followers and pushed too far by others. Dewey, himself, had warned his followers against assuming that he had the final answer and against developing his doctrine into a cult. He stated that he wanted an educational program based on experimentation and experience, one that would be ever changing.

Dewey's philosophy was much closer to that of the typical American— of the American whose watchword is "success"—than was that of his critics. He believed in pragmatism—what will work is truth and the truth is to be tested by its practical consequences. Even one of his severest critics, Herman H. Horn, said of Dewey's pragmatism:

> Pragmatism is practical, functional, near-to-earth, human, social. It is an educational philosophy that is improving school practice, making learning a more purposeful process, giving children a sense of reality in the school.

There is little doubt, however, that in a sense some followers of "progressive education" had been victimized by their interpretation of Dewey's philosophy that every child is an individual with special talents and should have an opportunity to succeed. It was very easy to go from this sound idea to the extreme of letting pupils get by with low achievement. According to John Dewey's theory, a fine school program is one which leads pupils from an early interest in solving problems of an immediately localized and concrete sort to a more mature interest in solving abstract problems arising through intellectual curiosity. Unfortunately, many of his followers never taught anything but the concrete, practical, and nontheoretical.

The freedom of expression and cultivation of individuality desired by Dewey has never been given more than a limited trial in educational experimentation. While the little creativity that the schools have stimulated is largely due to the "progressive education" movement, it has been so ridiculed that only the boldest educators have dared to fully try it. While a public school before Sputnik might have got by with many low-achieving students, it would have been unable to survive as a tax-supported institution had it granted much freedom of expression and encouraged much intellectual individuality. Those isolated schools that did give it a try often did not realize that to do original thinking a pupil must first find out what is the best thinking of his elders and then try to improve on it. Imposition from above is one thing; to think in a vacuum is impossible. The real originators "work up to a meaning and a tone and a signature of their own" by building on the past. They know that "what is past is prologue."

Dewey wanted to replace external discipline with free activity. Although an educated mind doesn't need external discipline the child is not educated. Yet one doesn't learn to direct his own life by being required continually to act in a certain pattern. Just as a teacher can go too far with forced discipline of pupils, so he can go to an extreme with freedom. When a child is given freedom before he has the knowledge and ability to use it, the result is usually anarchy. In the few so-called "progressive" schools anarchy was sometimes the pattern. A better balanced program was needed.

Dewey opposed learning from only textbooks and authorities at the period when such learning was the only pattern used in schools. Many of his followers, however, in a period when books and authorities were not held in such awe, killed much of the desire in children to read and to listen to anyone who by long work and study had become a specialist in his own field. They did not realize that experiences through reading and listening can be as worthwhile as any other experiences.

Dewey wanted learning of high quality. He was among the first educational thinkers in America to realize the necessity for motivation if there is to be quality learning. He believed that learning is best when there is not external drill, but the pupils have ends in view which make a direct vital appeal to them. This is the ideal. Too often "progressive educators" cut out the drills, even the hard work, without giving pupils a reason for learning on their own. Many such teachers had learned only about eliminating drill work, not the positive part of the progressive doctrine concerned with "ends in view."

But what is the answer? Is "progressive education" good or bad? I would say that in the long run it will be for the good. It has already broken the lock-step in American education which had been copied from Europe. It made possible the founding of a truly American system of education closely resembling the democratic ideals of this nation rather than the autocratic ideals of the economic elite who dominate European education to this very day. The ideas of "progressive education" vitalized American education. It has now been demonstrated that learning need not always be dull and boring; it can be vital, alive, and interesting.

What we must now find is a philosophy of education that provides a balance: that speaks of rights of adults as well as rights of children, of responsibilities as well as rights, of the abstract as well as the concrete, of the needs of society as well as the needs of the individual, of the need to make work enjoyable when possible, but realizing that pupils must sometimes do work that is dull, routine, and unchallenging.

We Americans must ever strive to improve our educational system. We must not be led down the path toward more authoritarianism in our public school program. In a democracy children must be taught responsible self-direction. They can learn this neither through a school system that is authoritarian nor through one that is in a state of anarchy.

Some of the critics of present day education, I am afraid, have been motivated by their guilt complexes derived from having frittered away their own time in school. Now they want to punish the child for the sins of the father. In the words of L. Pearsall Smith, "Criticizing youth is necessary for the good health of their elders. It increases their blood circulation." Just the same, we need the objective of which Robert Frost spoke when he said: "A lot of people are being scared by the Russians into hardening up our educational system or speeding it up. I am interested in toning it up."

In saying that "progressive education" has been both good *and* bad, I do not believe I have straddled the fence. I have stated my opinion as to when it has done more good than harm and when more harm than good.

"Progressive education" was the new idea in education at the turn of the century. What we need today is a better idea. Returning to the old is not the answer. Americans, including those in academic positions, are prone to place the "respectable" on their highest pedestal. Unfortunately, the new idea is seldom respectable. As leaders of thought, teachers have a duty to encourage rather than stifle those who have turned away from trying to fit yesterday's solutions to the problems of this changing world. Let's not just be unafraid of the new, but actively work in creating a fresh approach to our educational problems. The future of the nation greatly depends on the outcome of such an effort.

WARREN MILLER

The Field Trip

> . . . an down on the floor these men was running aroun with little
> bits of paper an yellin like they was a rumble on.

In his novel The Cool World *Warren Miller tells the story of an adolescent boy in Harlem and his rise to the leadership of his gang. Duke is engaged throughout most of the novel in proving himself by getting a gun for the gang to use in its fights, the "piece" referred to in this excerpt. The story of the class field trip not only serves to illustrate the theoretical value materials in the preceding articles, but also is a caustic expression of the total alienation of the slum child from the school and its values. The boys' attitude toward the teacher and trip is not hostile; Duke seems to like Mr. Shapiro. They simply are indifferent to his purposes and involved in their own affairs. Miller seems to be saying in this chapter, and in the novel as a whole, that what is valuable about the world of the gang is that the boys find status and recognition in it. If he is correct, what can the school do to substitute for it?*

Three big buses lined up waitin. Mister Shapiro say "Custis. Summer. You almost missed the outing. Line up now boys."

We go to the bus with a card stuck to the door sayin

8th Grade
Mr. Shapiro

an we got on. Handy savin me a seat up front. "You get it?" He say. An then the others stick they faces over the back of my seat. "You get it Duke?" They all askin.

Mr. Shapiro get on the bus. He say. "All right boys. Now I know we are going to enjoy this trip."

So we go down to Wall Street that day Mister Shapiro he took us. Shapiro is okay he aint always yellen at us like the rest of them. Some of

From Warren Miller, *The Cool World*, Boston, 1959, pp. 5, 12–17. Copyright © 1959 by Warren Miller, reprinted by permission of Little, Brown and Co.

the teachers tell you. "Stay out. Dont come to school an we wont report you. You co operate with me an I will co operate with you." They dont want to be bothered. Mister Shapiro he aint like that. A little man. He look worried all the time. Got lines in his forhead like they been cut in.

First we went to the George Washington Museum. It has this big statue of him out front. The place where we went was the cellar of this building where they got cases full of things from histry. Mister Shapiro he lead us around explainin this an that. Histry make Mister Shapiro get all hopped up you know. He say. "Think of it boys where you standen right now maybe the Father of our Country once stood." Evrybody look down at they feet.

Handy and Summer an me was in the back an all they talken about was the piece. Handy say. "Shitman you get yourself a piece you gonna be President of the Crocadiles. Aint no doubt about that."

"Where you hear that?" I ask him.

He just shrug. He just shrug. "Hear it around." He say. "Blood is getten old. He gonna be 20 soon. He cant swing with the gang for ever. Time he moved up."

Summer say to me. "Whut kind of piece you say it was Duke man?" Summer talk like a big shot because his father a big man in the numbers.

I tell him it was a Colt.

"Birettas is better." Summer say.

Handy say. "Dint Priest spread the word whut he had was a Biretta?"

"That whut he say. But whut he got is a Colt." I tell him.

"I like the Biretta my self." Summer say.

"Biretta the best Duke." Handy tell me. "That is one sweet piece the Biretta."

"I like the Biretta." Summer say.

"Biretta is for women." I tell them.

"Now hold on Man." Summer say. "Now jus a minute. Lemme tell you something Man. Colt dont have the improvements Man. Why shitman them Colts is the same motheren piece they was usen at Cussers Last Stan."

Then Handy get into it. Like he knew whut he talken about you know. He say. "The man is right."

"Improvements." I say. "Shitman you can take those improvements. I want a piece I can be sure of. Colt is sure. Lemme ask you somethin Man lemme ask you somethin. Why you think the headbreakers usen a Colt if it no good? Let me ask you that Summer? Man you got Biretta on the brain. You dont have the bread to buy a cap pistol an all you talken is Biretta."

"The Man is right." Handy say. Meanin me. That I am right.

Summer say. "Shitman the reason headbreakers usen the Colt is because they dont know no better. Thats all."

Mister Shapiro he call us over. He tell us not to get lost an stay with the class. Then he say. "Just think boys. This is the place where George Washington tooken the Oath of Office an become our first president."

"Now whut do you think of that." Someone say.

Mister Shapiro dont pay no attention to him. He say. "Do you never think boys that they was a time this nation of ours was just *one day old?*"

"Jus a goddamn baby." Same person say. George Cadmus. Mister Shapiro know but he dont pay any atention. He talken about how rough things was in the old days. Man it was rough at Valley Forge an places like that he tellin us.

Then we walk aroun an look at the sords an things like that from history an then Mister Shapiro tooken us across the street to the stock exchange. They got these little streets down in that part of town. On one corner they was a man a white man wearin a derby hat tellin a crowd of people about the Bible an they was hecklin him. He was standin on a box with the American Flag painted on it. Some of the guys lit up butts while we was crossin the street an Mister Shapiro made out like he dint notice.

We went into this big bilding then an befor we got on the elevator Mister Shapiro made evrybody throw away his butts. He knew we was smoken. Then we went up to the stock exchange and looked at the exhibits about the City of the Future. These rocket ships kept flyin back an forth over it. They were on wires you could see the wires. An the City of Future it was jus a big housing projek. If you wanted to know whut it all about they had these phones an you could listen in.

When you picked up the phone you could hear this TV announcer tellin you how much steel they gonna need to bild the City of the Future. George Cadmus was breaden everybody up. He standen there with the phone saying things like. "Uh huh. You dont say Man. Well uh listen Man how things in Pittsberg?" Like this TV announcer was talken to him.

Then we looked at other exibits about tires an aluminum and then we went inta this big room. We was up on a little balcony an down on the floor these men was running aroun with little bits of paper an yellin like they was a rumble on. Hangin on the wall was the biggest American Flag I ever see any where.

Then it was time for the movie and we all went in to this little movie and saw a movie about America. It show rivers an factories & farms & mountains & a workinman in a blue shirt buyin stocks. Flash Gordon he was sittin in front of me slash the back of a seat with his blade and all the stuffin started fallin out. An Lonesome Pine unscrewed the arm of his chair with a dime. When the lights went on we made a lot of noise and Mister Shapiro hussled us out an never noticed the damage.

On the way out they give us these little books about how we could own a Share of America an about how to organize a club an buy these stocks.

When we got out to the street the bus driver threw his butt away and he say. "All right. This bus was hire for 2 hours and the time is up." An he got in an drive off. Mister Shapiro took us back up town on the subway.

So that was the last day of school an summer started.

"Mees, You Goin' to Be Real Teacher Now, Don' Cha?"

I look up. It is 8 o'clock; there is a roaring in the corridors and a sudden flood of children into the classroom. The small, brown boy who approaches my desk eyes me eagerly.

"Yes, I'm the regular teacher, and I hope to stay for the rest of the year. You've had three teachers already, haven't you?"

"Yes, Mees, dey all leavin' because we fightin'. For you we not goin' to fight." He flings himself into a seat and sits at attention.

"What's your name?"

"Me name ees Andres an' I already know you name is Mees Parkhair."

"Que bueno!" I laugh.

"Mees!" Andres starts up in alarm, "Don' let dem hear you speakin' Spanish. You get in lots of troble. We go to office, get boom, boom when we say one ting in Spanish. You be careful, Mees." Suddenly his face registers delight and he leans across his desk with a conspiratorial whisper —"You *know* Spanish, Mees?"

"Si, amiguito, vivimas cinco anos en Mexico," ("Yes, my friend, we lived five years in Mexico.") I stand up, speaking slowly and distinctly. "The reason they don't want you to speak Spanish is that they hope you will practice your English. But I need to practice my Spanish—so we can practice on each other, O.K.? That way, we'll all learn."

I Borrow You Mine

There are 24 boys and girls caught here in the lowest section of third grade. They can go no lower. The first two grades are in another school. Four or five are in this class because their families have returned late from their migrations. The rest are the castoffs of the other two sections of third grade, dumped on the teacher whose section has been made up

Ann Parker, " 'Mees, You Goin' to Be Real Teacher Now, Don' Cha?' " *American Education*, May, 1967.

last. Their ages range from nine to sixteen. Their handicaps range from mental deficiency to almost no previous schooling to emotional blocks to physical weakness. None of them understands much English.

Many of them are not stupid, but not one has been tested to determine his potential abilities or the reasons for failure. They have merely been exposed to third grade work and found wanting. I have been handed a stack of third grade texts, marked at the place where the last teacher left off, and told: "Do the best you can—this is the worst bunch in the school."

Alcario, one of the smallest boys in the class, comes in, pockets bulging with hard-earned money. He works every day after school and all day Saturday. Today he takes his money and buys seven chocolate milks, marching gravely around the room and placing them with great dignity on the desks of his friends.

Cold rain has left the kids soaked and shivering at the opening of school. Andres huddles in his seat when the others go out to physical education. "I too wet, too cold to go." Oswaldo swaggers by (he always swaggers), peels off his jacket, and holds it out to Andres. "I borrow you mine." This is typical. Lending, giving, and treating are as natural as breathing for these children.

From the first day of school I have confused Lorenzo with Oswaldo. They have finally come to answer matter-of-factly to either name. Today I call on Lorenzo (calling him Oswaldo) and he beings to recite. When he cannot complete the recitation, Oswaldo breaks in to help him. I snap, "Is your name Oswaldo?" to which he replies meekly. "Si, Senora." How does one maintain a straight face in these moments? The class waits only long enough to be sure that I am going to laugh, and bursts into uproarious guffaws.

———

Rana is fourteen and cannot read. The little boys look up to him because he is big and tough. He brags that he has been in jail for theft and that he spends his weekends drunk. He is the only member of the class that I have to force myself to like.

One day, two dollars disappear from my drawer. It is the money the children have paid to see a musical program. I see Rana watching me carefully. An investigation satisfies me that he has taken the money. Privately, I tell him to replace it by the following morning. Nothing is said to the class except that the money will be restored. Rana brings the money the next morning. From that day he is my friend.

Once when I leave the key to my desk drawer at home, and can't open it, Rana volunteers. "Oh dat too easy," and in less than a minute he picks the lock. I thank him admiringly, and he sits down, gratified.

Which Weetch?

Sign on the principal's door: "May we have courage to change what can be changed, patience to endure what can't be changed, and wisdom to know the difference." Very apropos! I have been in to ask why we don't teach the kids to read in Spanish first. Impossible. Why don't we hire Latin teachers? They wouldn't command respect. Why don't we use textbooks that have content interesting to children of this age and background? Well, we might, if I knew of any. Why don't we test the children when they enter to find out what level they can work on? The practice has been to test them at the end to see what they've learned (or failed to learn).

———

The reading lab packets arrived today. They are on a third grade level. We can't use any of it. Maybe I can request some first grade packets.

I eventually get some second grade kits and they are a great joy to the three or four kids who are able to use them. I can't seem to convince anyone that we really need first grade kits.

———

The children love to go to the library. They come back hugging books with wonderful pictures and begging, "Here, Mees, you read dees one now." They thrust their books upon me, eager to know all that the pictures mean.

Danielito waves a book, his eyes sparkling: "Look, Mees, one Wanderfool Weezard of Oz! Eet have a weetch. Maybe you know eet?"

"Yes, I saw the movie about the Wizard of Oz when I was little."

Joe Salinas chimes in eagerly: "Oh, I know eet too! I see eet too! I weetch you a merry Chreestmas!"

"Well, that's something else; that's *wish*."

"No, Mees! I weetch you a merry Chreestmas, dat's what eet say."

So it goes. When I ask them what jam is, someone insists it is where big boys play basketball. The word "watch" is the same as "wash," and "sad" and "sat" are alike. One poem has the line, "Especially on Christmas week, temptation is so great to peek." I notice laughter every time we say this line. I wonder if it could be one of the innumerable "bad words" whose innocent use always brings laughter. Finally I ask, and Javier chortles, "Oh, Mees, peek tomatoes!"

What a "great blooming, buzzing confusion" the English language is to these kids! If they can't hear it and can't say it, how do we expect them to read it and write it?

Da Beegest Pencil

I use the Spanish word "mies" for "harvest." None of the children knows the word. Nor do they know the word "cosecha" (crop). They simply use "campo," which means field, or more often the name of whatever fruit or vegetable is being picked. There are a great many Spanish words which they do not know. What they will speak eventually is "Tex-Mex," a patois formed by jumbling broken English and broken Spanish together. This will enable them to live in the world of the migrant worker, and no other. Instead of being bilingual, they will, in a sense, be nonlingual, for their language is not a recognized language. The worlds of literature and history and political science and the arts are closed to them.

It is a shock to realize that after all the traveling they've done, these kids have no idea where they are or where they've been; no concept of distance, direction, or the relation of one place to another. Now we are working with a large wall map which I brought from home. They love it. It doesn't require much reading, and they are quite sharp about remembering places once they are pointed out. Some do much better than others, of course, but at least no one thinks that Africa is in Illinois any more!

Andres says gleefully: "What ees da beegest pencil?" No one knows. "Pennsylvania!" Everyone loves this joke, because by now we know where Pennsylvania is.

We Movin' All Da Time

The day we change rooms is one to remember. Our room is very hot and there is a shady one standing vacant down the hall. So I announce, "Kids, we are moving out." They snap to atttention like hounds that have picked up a scent. "Not to Illinois, not in a car or truck; we're moving down the hall to that empty room, just as quickly and quietly as we can."

It is like throwing a switch. One moment all is intense listening. The next moment, a whirlwind has struck. Maps fall from the walls, books disappear from the shelves, my dask drawers are seen departing out the door; all I can do is run after them.

Within the hour every bit of equipment is in place in the new room; the maps and cards and decorations are on the walls, the kids are erect and proud in their seats. I look over the neat rows and ask, "Where on earth did you learn to work like that?" Rana, sweat still dripping from his face, answers joyfully, "Oh, Mees, dat how we know to work. We movin' all da time." Yes, Rana, moving, and working in the fields, working as I have never worked. Too bad we don't have achievement tests for that.

———

Mario is fourteen. He is well built and does a man's work and receives a man's wages. He has been a cotton picker all his life. He cannot read because he has never been in school long enough to learn. I see him before the class, his big hands gripping the elementary reader with painful intensity. His brow is furrowed; he is working hard. "See Puff run. Funny, funny Puff."

I remember the sudden awareness in Mario's eyes yesterday when I mentioned communism. I think how seldom he smiles. He struggles on with Puff and Dick and Jane. He is a good boy, never a discipline problem. I try to imagine what fires of resentment must burn behind the quiet face. Dear God, send us books for boys like Mario! (When our reader about the frontiersman finally arrives, Mario has already moved on.)

Pedro He Ees My Boy

Visitors' Day. We have worked like mad decorating the room and arranging exhibits. By the end of the day, everything is beautiful and the workbooks, decorated with brightly colored butterflies, adorn the desks.

At 8 o'clock, I am all ready to receive the parents. The school is blazing with lights, and charged with that festive air which accompanies a gathering in a place of work during hours that are not work hours. Most of the teachers are dressed to the hilt. I am not. No one comes.

Finally, a huge, sunburned man peers shyly through the door. He has a crumpled list in his hand, which he refers to anxiously. He is Pedro's father.

"Pedro he ees my boy. How he do een school? He no giving you trouble?"

"Not at all. Pedro sits right here by my desk, and he is my special friend. Look at the work he has there. See how neatly he writes."

The father's face brightens as he looks over his son's work. Yes, it is neat. Pedro must be all right.

Out of thirty-four students (our enrollment at the peak of the season), four parents have come to visit. I am disappointed for the children's sake as well as for my own. Perhaps though, the children didn't really expect them to come. The fathers look so uncomfortable in their "dress-up" clothes, and how can they talk with teachers most of whom speak only

English? No, it is better for them to keep away from the school and hope the children stay out of trouble.

———

Of all the teachers' meetings we are asked to attend, one is eminently worthwhile. The chief speaker is a Negro educator from Chicago. He begins his address in Persian, switches to Oxford English, and finally lapses into Texas talk. The teachers get the message. He points out the simple fact that Latin kids do not learn from us primarily because we are not speaking their language.

After the meeting, I seek him out and begin to unburden my soul. He soon interrupts me: "Shut your door, throw the damn textbooks out, and teach those kids what you think they need to know." I never feel completely hopeless after this day.

———

The achievement tests have been taken and sent in. It is a farce. Most of my kids will remain in third grade—why push them into fourth grade readers and workbooks? It is too easy for teachers to hate children who can't keep up with the class. I wish they could be in an ungraded room with no failure threat hanging over their heads.

———

Our books are turned back and the year is over. Tomorrow I will bring the tape recorder and record messages from all the kids. Of course, I have their school pictures, but the tapes will be nice.

The kids are eager to help set up the tape recorder. First I make a farewell speech and play it back so that they will know what they are about to do. I tell them how wonderful they are and that I will never forget them. Some day, somewhere, we will have a happy meeting. The children are either crying or laughing at those who are crying. Alfredo sobs, "Eef you ask me what I like best, I was gonna say you."

The kids make their speeches and I say good-bye again. They all leave, except Pedro. He stands close to my desk: "I don't tink I g-gonna leave yet. I s-stay here awhile m-more w-weeth you, Mees."

"Pedro, I have to go." I slam the windows down and lock them, turn off the lights, kiss the top of Pedro's head and shove him into the hall. He walks away very slowly. Blindly, I make for the parking lot. The year is over and the children are gone.

Can Johnny Read?

Teaching children to read is the most important single responsibility of the schools because all further education depends upon it, and a nation of illiterates can neither govern itself nor maintain itself as a civilized society.

All schools accept this responsibility, but in recent years the educational world has been torn by bitter controversy over the soundness of our reading programs and the quality of the results. The conflict came to public attention with the publication in 1955 of Rudolf Flesch's "Why Johnny Can't Read." The latest attack is "Tommorow's Illiterates," sponsored by the Council for Basic Education.

The critics are convinced that reading instruction has gone to pot— that children today read less well than their ancestors, that the methods used in most of our schools are faulty, and that the blame lies with the educationists who have discouraged the teaching of phonics and have watered down the literary content of the textbooks used in our elementary schools.

Professional educators who defend the status quo insist that reading is taught better today than ever before, that the methods used in most of our schools are sound, and that the critics don't know what they are talking about. Obviously someone is badly mistaken.

The debaters cannot agree even on what they mean by "reading"— whether it is the art of identifying and pronouncing words or the ability to get meaning from a printed page. Nor do they agree about the basic facts that must underlie any sound program of reading instruction. Some critics contend that the average child has a vocabulary of 10,000 or more words when he enters school and needs only to learn to recognize and pronounce them when he sees them in print. But many professional educators estimate the child's vocabulary at a much lower figure—some put it as low as 2,500 words—and insist that a long period of "reading readiness," including vocabulary building, must precede reading instruction. When the experts are so far apart in their interpretation of the definitions and the

Paul Woodring, "Can Johnny Read?" *Saturday Review*, January 20, 1962.

basic facts (both sides cite "research" evidence) it is difficult for the layman to have much confidence in either group.

He cannot easily choose on the basis of the professional qualifications of the protagonists. The defense of the present system is led by professional educators who have devoted their lives to research in reading. On the other hand, Rudolf Flesch, foremost and most strident of the critics, holds a doctor's degree from Columbia's Teachers College and he too has spent many years studying the problems of reading. Other critics are university professors of English, and elementary reading teachers of long experience who report great success in their own classrooms with Flesch's phonics method or some variant of it.

Both groups write a great deal but they do not really communicate. The education professors write for professional journals which are not widely read even by teachers. The critics write for more general public— their articles have appeared in many popular magazines and their books, notably *Why Johnny Can't Read*, have sold by the hundreds of thousands. The professional educators write scathing denunciations of these popular books and find many errors in them but do not come squarely to grips with their central arguments. The critics, on the other hand, are prone to ignore the evidence offered by the educators. The arguments presented by the two sides bypass each other.

For the past year we have been trying to find, for our readers, a definitive article, written by someone able to stand above the fray, survey the facts calmly, tell us what it is all about, and advise parents, teachers, and school board members regarding what steps might be taken to improve the teaching of reading. We have been unable to find such an article. We receive many manuscripts on reading but all the authors who are informed on the subject seem to have chosen up sides and to have become polemicists better able to lash out than to evaluate. We do not think that further publication of polemics, on either side, is likely to lead to a solution of the problem, or even to its clarification.

We are not experts on the teaching of reading and do not profess to have read more than a small part of the vast literature on the subject. But we have read enough and have heard and seen enough to have reached some tentative conclusions:

By any reasonable definition of reading the great majority of boys and girls today can and do read. If "Johnny" is taken to mean an average American child, the charge that "Johnny can't read" is arrant nonsense. He can and he does.

A sizable minority of American children—no one really knows how many but estimates run to several million—reach the age of ten or twelve, and some reach high school, without being able to read well enough to qualify as literates. Because of lack of reliable data we do not know, with any degree of certainty, whether the percentage is increasing but there is ample evidence that nonreaders have always been with us and that they are found in all lands. Until education became compulsory the schools dealt with them by failing them and letting them drop out at an early age; but this solution is no longer possible and the result is that more of them now reach the upper grades where their limitations are more obvious.

The widely heard charge that average reading ability has declined over the years must be labeled "unproved." There is not enough evidence to affirm or deny it. Such evidence as we have (none of it is based upon an adequate national sampling with comparable tests for the different periods) is conflicting and confused and has been interpreted differently by different people. The bulk of it seems to suggest that there has been some improvement in reading over the years but not as much as might have been predicted from the fact that the school year now is longer and teachers are better prepared.

The important question is not whether Johnny reads better than his ancestors but whether he reads as well as he needs to and can learn to. We think the answer to this is a firm no. With better instruction the average performance can rise higher than it has ever been and the number of failures can be greatly reduced.

Reading should be defined as the ability to comprehend the author's meaning. Learning to identify and pronounce words is only the first step.

There is no one correct or sound method of learning to read. Successful teachers have always employed a variety of methods, children have learned to read in many different ways, and many very bright children can read before they enter school. Enthusiasts for any one of the many systems which they have themselves invented can demonstrate remarkable results with their own children in their own classrooms because any of several methods will yield good results when used by a brilliant teacher devoted to her work. It does not follow that the same system should be universally adopted because it is far from certain that it will be equally effective with average teachers.

Any sound system must include a way of attacking unfamiliar words. Until about 1925 this was provided for by the formal teaching of phonics but new procedures emerged which de-emphasized phonics and included this approach only informally and when the teacher thought it was needed. Whatever may have been the intention of the reading specialists, it now seems clear that a great many teachers somehow got the impression that phonics was old-fashioned, and hence, bad. The result was that many of the children who learned to read during the 1930's and 1940's learned no phonics at all of too little to be useful. Some of these are now teachers.

The efforts of some educators to discount phonics on the basis of "new discoveries in psychology" are based on specious reasoning and are not justified by Gestalt psychology or any other kind of psychology. It is true that an experienced reader grasps ideas rapidly from words or phrases as a whole. He pauses to analyze only when he encounters an unfamiliar word. But, to the child learning to read, many words are unfamiliar and a knowledge of phonics is essential. It should be included in every reading program and should be commenced early. It is not sound for the teacher to postpone phonics "until the child needs it" because, when he needs it, the teacher may not be present to help him.

One the child gets past the initial hurdles of learning to read, the material presented to him should be real literature. It should be selected in terms of his level of comprehension but the classics should not be re-written to fit a word count for when they are rewritten they are no longer classics. Reading should be an elevating experience—one that permits the spirit to soar. There are numerous selections from great literature, and from scientific and political papers, that can be understood by children and these should be read in the original. It is not essential that the child understand every word; he will broaden his vocabulary by meeting new words in the context of familiar ones.

The reading teacher of demonstrated competence should hold an honored place in the academic hierarchy and should be given freedom and responsibility comparable to that afforded the college professor. She should be free to use whatever methods she finds most successful with her own pupils. She must accept responsibility for results, but we do not think it wise to allow any single rigid system in instruction to be imposed by supervisors, research specialists, textbook makers, or anyone else.

All elementary teachers should be carefully selected, broadly educated, and professionally prepared, but even with this selection and education some will teach reading much better than others. Team teaching will make it possible for the successful ones to extend their talents to more children by spending less time on duties requiring a lesser degree of professional skill. Non-graded primary schools will make it possible for a reading teacher to work with the same children for more than one year.

Reading should not be a battleground. We hope that the specialists and critics of many persuasions will climb down from their barricades and quit taking pot shots at each other. If they will read more carefully themselves many of them will discover that they have been misinterpreting what their opponents are trying to say. We hope that they will regain their sense of balance, examine all the evidence more carefully, and quit beclouding the issues with wild charges and extravagant claims.

J. A. BATTLE

The Content of Method
and the Method of Content

Our Western culture has been plagued for centuries by an "either-or" philosophy which has created a strong tendency to see everything in the society as either black or white with no shades of gray. And educators of the Western world have been victimized by this philosophy almost as badly as the average citizen, for they have made their dichotomies in academic society on the issues of "breadth and depth" and "method and content."

Many arguments have ensued between those who uphold "method" and those who champion "content." These arguments, especially when the education of teachers for the American public schools is at issue, have sometimes been as intense as those which have been made throughout history in the area of religious dogmas. It is possible that some instructors in colleges of liberal arts and education alike have had to turn to emotion to try to get their points across because of their lack of clear thinking on this problem.

Good teachers know their subject and good teachers possess a distinctive body of knowledge concerned with the art and science of teaching. Teachers who do not know content are not educated persons, and if they do not have a knowledge of professional subject matter (method) which is distinctive from that possessed by others, they have no more right to make decisions which concern education than any other educated persons.

Content may be learned apart from a method of teaching, but a method of teaching, except in the abstract, cannot be separated from content. Content and method in teacher education are inseparable because method is the *application of content*. Yet so-called experts in teacher education often attempt to make a sharp distinction between the two when, in fact, they are both a part of the same pattern.

This article was inspired by a conversation with a fine teacher educator who drew an incorrect, in my opinion, dichotomy in a good teacher education program between content and method. We were talking with him about the few students who get through teacher education programs in

151

every institution in the nation with very high grades but who probably should not be certified to teach because they have authoritarian type personalities. The educator remarked that possibly programs in teacher education "which emphasize content" turn out more of this type of student than the usual program "which emphasizes methods."

I had thought that he understood our programs in teacher education at the University of South Florida, so I was amazed at his statement for two reasons. First, we have stated repeatedly in our teacher education programs that we put equal emphasis on method and content and that we do not believe this to be a matter of either-or but of both-and. We are not only interested in the "what" of content and the "how" of method but want our students to know the "why" of each. As a result in our elementary specialization courses, for instance, we have teachers who are experts both in their subject fields and in the understanding of how to teach them in the elementary school context. Secondly, I was amazed at his implication that a "method oriented" program would eliminate the "authoritarian types." In my opinion, such an unrealistic type of course perpetuates the problem rather than solves it. Because the methods are taught in a vacuum the "authoritarian types" do not have to get in touch with reality. They can continue to try to make their own reality. Also, in the so-called "method oriented" courses I haven't seen many students of any philosophy or achievement level who did not make the grade.

It was shocking to find that we had failed to communicate to our friend our philosophy here of emphasizing content and method *together*. The selection of courses to be taught by the College of Education, we want to emphasize, is not made on whether they are content or methods courses. In fact, our students take only one three-trimester-hour course which is labeled a "methods" course, and even it is not "pure." So if we made this type of division we in the College of Education would be almost out-of-business. The philosophy which we use at this university for making decisions on whether a course belongs in the College of Education or not is one that has every historical precedent. When colleges of education first came into being they taught the courses for teachers which were not being taught by the liberal arts colleges. This is exactly where we stand today. There is no need for a college of education to duplicate a course that is being offered to students, including teacher candidates, by the other colleges of the university. However, a course designed only for teachers should be taught by the college of education. Thus, a general speech course which teacher candidates might take would not be offered by our College of Education, but it might offer a special course with the title "Speech for Teachers." Since most of the courses for students in the teaching specialization fields of secondary education are also offered to other students in the university by the other colleges they would never be a part of the College of Education offerings. In this area it is the function of the College of Education, together with the University Council on Teacher Education, to help to coordinate these courses in the total teacher education program. On the other hand, courses for students in the teaching specialization fields of elementary education are designed principally for teachers and are therefore offered in the College of Education.

Finally, as to our philosophy on "method versus subject-matter issue" we want to state that when we speak of method we are talking about everything (and we do mean everything—all the knowledge) that the teacher utilizes to get the pupil better educated. This controversy between content and method reminds me of a saying of Shailer Mathews: "An epigram is a half-truth so stated as to irritate the persons who believe the other half."

"Universities are full of knowledge; the freshmen bring a little in and the seniors take none away, and knowledge accumulates."

—A. LAWRENCE LOWELL

LUCY TROXELL

On Socrates, Who Warned Us of the Danger of Becoming Misanthropists (Haters of Men) and Misologists (Haters of Ideas)

He was an awkward man with a pot-belly, a short neck, a thick nose, a bald head, and protruding eyes and was married to a woman whose speech brought as little pleasure to her listeners as his looks brought to his viewers. He once jokingly explained: "As I intended to associate with all kinds of people, I had accustomed myself to bear the disposition of Xantippe."

Socrates was born in the outskirts of Athens about 496 B.C. He became a great soldier who was commended for his bravery, a Senator noted for his integrity, a most sociable man who delighted his friends equally with his witticisms and with his expressions of profound wisdom, and a philosopher who walked the streets of Athens barefooted trying to stir up the people to examine their lives. He had as his theme: The greatest good of man is daily to converse about virtue and the life which is unexamined is not worth living.

Socrates believed that if the citizens of Athens would examine their lives honestly that they would put less value on money, honor, and reputation and would put more value on wisdom, truth, and improvement of the soul. At the age of 70 he was brought to trial by his fellow citizens not so much for what he had said to them but for having deflated so many of their philosophical pretensions. He exposed as pompous frauds many men in high places, claiming that he was better off than they because they knew nothing and thought they knew and "I neither know nor think that I know." Many of those he exposed became his enemies. Since they were pretentious people they did not accuse him of fracturing their ego. Instead they accused him of creating new gods and corrupting the youth. It never crossed their minds that the one who commits the greatest impiety and who is the greatest corrupter of youth is the hypocrite.

At his trial Socrates stated he was "a sort of gadfly, given to the State by the Gods; and that the State is like a great and noble steed who is tardy in his motions owing to his very size, and required to be stirred into life." He advised the Athenians that he had neglected all of his own concerns for years so that he could come to them like a father or elder brother to exhort them to take care of their greatest need which is virtue. He said he was economically impoverished because he had given so much time to his self-appointed responsibility of "arousing and persuading and reproaching" the citizens of Athens. He advised the Athenians, for their own welfare, to spare his life "as you will not easily find another like me." Without another gadfly like him, he said, they would sleep on for the remainder of their lives. Possibly because they wanted to sleep for the remainder of their lives Socrates' fellow citizens sentenced him to die.

On the day Socrates was to die by drinking hemlock poison he spent his time calmly discussing philosophical issues with his friends. In the midst of the conversation he was asked a question. Before he answered it he said he wanted to hear what his friend Crito was going to say to him. "Only this, Socrates," replied Crito, "The attendant who is to give you the poison has been telling me that you are not to talk much, and he wants me to let you know this; for that by talking heat is increased, and this interferes with the action of the poison; those who excite themselves are sometimes obliged to drink the poison two or three times."

"Then," said Socrates, "let him mind his business and be prepared to give the poison two or three times, if necessary; that is all."

The great authority on Stoic morals, Epictetus, who was a Greek but who was taken to Rome as a slave during the reign of Nero, agreed with Socrates that the beginning of philosophy is to know one's own mind. He said that because Socrates had constantly subjected his life to examination, he could say, when told to prepare for his trial, "Thinkest thou not that I have been preparing for it all my life?" His questioner persisted:

"In what way?"

"I have maintained that which in me lay."

"How so?"

"I have never, secretly or openly, done a wrong unto any."

Socrates left nothing in writing. What we know of his teachings we learn principally from his disciples, Xenophon and Plato. Plato's works take the form of dialogues, in which if Plato appears it is only as a listener, and in which the main speaker is Socrates. Since Plato developed the philosophy of Socrates apparently far beyond the point reached by Socrates himself, it is impossible to make a correct judgment on how much of his writings are Socrates' and how much are Plato's. But whether the writings are those of the master or those of the pupil they nevertheless are filled with both sense and nonsense. While Thomas Jefferson may have been the first American to point out publicly the nonsene in Plato's writings, almost any school boy or girl can discover this simply by reading the conversation related by Plato between Socrates and his friends on his last day in prison. In this conversation Socrates agrees that a person acquires *before* birth his knowledge of the ideals of beauty, goodness, justice, and holiness. But dismissing Socrates because some of his *answers* are so inconsistent with what is known today about how knowledge is acquired is somewhat like dismissing him because he believed in the pagan gods instead of the God worshipped by the Christians or the Buddhists. Socrates lived before Christ and Buddha and therefore he could not possibly have been a Christian or a Buddhist. He lived, of course, before there was a psychology of learning and therefore anything he said about the acquiring of knowledge had to be no more than pure speculation. But what needs to be remembered about Socrates is that no one today is asking *questions* more relevant to our times than those he asked.

Socrates has meaning for us today, not only because he asked questions that are most relevant to our times but because of his devotion to *seeking* answers to such relevant questions as: What is truth? What is beauty? What is goodness? And he has meaning because he *acted* on a basis of the answers he found. Epictetus gave what he believed would be Socrates' answer to a question about pleasure: "But what says Socrates?—One man finds pleasure in improving his land, another his horses, my pleasure lies in seeing myself grow better day by day."

If the student who is preparing to become a teacher could derive his principal pleasure from "seeing that I myself grow better day by day" it is almost certain that his students would also learn to strive toward "the good life" sought by Socrates. Thus he would not be in danger of becoming a type of person that Socrates constantly warned his fellow Athenians to guard against becoming, misanthropists or haters of men and misologists or haters of ideas. Socrates believed that the hate of men and the hate of ideas spring from the same source which is, "ignorance of the world." And he said that to become a misologist is one of the worst things that can happen. In saying this, Socrates was giving an answer that is just as true today as it was in his ancient day.

JOHN GAUSS

Teacher Evaluation

Teacher: Socrates

A. Personal Qualifications

Rating
(high to low)
1 2 3 4 5

COMMENTS

1. Personal appearance

Dresses in an old sheet draped about his body.

2. Self-confidence

Not sure of himself—always asking questions.

3. Use of English

Speaks with a heavy Greek accent.

4. Adaptability

Prone to suicide by poison when under duress.

B. Class Management

1. Organization

Does not keep a seating chart.

2. Room appearance

Does not have eye-catching bulletin boards.

3. Utilization of supplies

Does not use supplies.

C. Teacher-Pupil Relationships

1. Tact and consideration

Places students in embarrassing situation by asking questions.

2. Attitude of class

Class is friendly.

John Gauss, "Teacher Evaluation," *Phi Delta Kappan,* January, 1962.

D. Techniques of Teaching

1. Daily preparation

Does not keep daily lesson plans.

2. Attention to course of study

Quite flexible—allows students to wander to different topics.

3. Knowledge of subject matter

Does not know material —has to question pupils to gain knowledge.

E. Professional Attitude

1. Professional ethics

Does not belong to professional association or PTA.

2. In-service training

Complete failure here— has not even bothered to attend college.

3. Parent relationships

Needs to improve in this area—parents are trying to get rid of him.

RECOMMENDATION: Does not have a place in education—should not be rehired.

MARGARET BENNETT

Teaching Is Better With!

Margaret Bennett is a teacher in the Los Angeles public schools. She writes that although the name is "the nom de machine à écrire which I use during my off hours, the events described in the article are absolutely true, and I have the lines between my eyes and gray hairs in my crown to prove it."

Hardly anyone these days has a good word to say for education courses. Teachers criticize them, student criticize them, university professors criticize them, and Admiral Rickover criticizes them. It's not uncommon to hear a Ph.D. in mathematics convulse the crowd at a cocktail party by pointing out that, since he has never taken an education course, he is not considered qualified to teach the multiplication table to fourth graders. Yes, among the informed, the consensus is that education courses are nothing but hurdles of boredom and worthlessness designed to keep intellectuals out of a profession where they are desperately needed.

I, too, once held this opinion. As an undergraduate majoring in English at UCLA, I sneered at my roommate who was taking the education courses required for an elementary teaching credential. I saw her patiently lettering "The ocean says 'Roar, roar,'" on a chart, strumming "Widdy Widdy Wicky, I Call My Pet Chickie" on the autoharp, and committing to memory such profound gems of philosophy as "In the main, children tend to be different." How, I often wondered could a rational human being spend even five seconds of precious existence on such senseless endeavors?

And then, in 1954, I graduated. This was at the height of the elementary teacher shortage in Southern California. The need was so acute that emergency credentials were being issued to anyone with a B.A., a negative chest X-ray, and a personal history free from any taint of Communism. Since I qualified, and since no one else was clamoring for my vague talents, I decided to become a teacher.

I approached my job with confidence. After all, I could read and write and handle arithmetic up to my twelvesies. . . . Besides that, since I had

Margaret Bennett, "Teaching Is Better With!" *Saturday Review*, February 16, 1963.

just spent four years in fresh, hot pursuit of truth and beauty, I would be able to give my students that something extra which the "educators" never could—a slight kiss of the gods, as it were.

My assignment was to a new school in the San Fernando Valley, where the enrollment had turned out to be double the anticipated number. When I reported for duty, a week after the semester started, there were three second-grade classes—all over the legal limit in size. A fourth was made up for me by taking ten or twelve children from each of the others. Naturally, any teacher in her right mind who has a chance to send children to another class will get rid of the pills. All three of the regular second-grade teachers were in their right minds. My class was, therefore, composed of the cream of the second-grade problem children plus some extra-low I.Q.'s (called "slow learners" in the trade).

Besides this ill-starred collection of students, I had an additional joy. The school was on half-day session to accommodate the unexpected hordes, and I drew an afternoon shift. My children attended class from 12:30 P.M. to 4:10 P.M. After a morning filled with roller skating and sibling battling, they were both keyed up and exhausted. This made for easy explosion of their already volatile personalities.

I would like to be able to relate in detail my first day in the classroom, but I have repressed it so completely that only several years of psychiatric probing could bring it to the surface again. I can, however, dredge up what would be a typical day in this, the grimmest period of my life.

I would arrive at school at noon, haggard from a night filled with the emotional breakdowns I could not allow myself in the classroom. The teacher who shared quarters with me released her class upon the world at 12:10, leaving me only twenty minutes to get ready for my onslaught of pupils.

By way of preparation, I would pace across the woven floor-sitting mat in the front of the room, wringing my hands, listening to the feet scurrying outside, waiting for the inevitable pounding on the door which indicated a pre-school fight or a parent bringing back a child who had been home storing up energy with a case of measles.

In the manner of Coué, I would chant to myself, "They're only little children. They're only *seven years* old. You're an intelligent adult. You can handle them." Then came the bell. My icy hand turned on the doorknob, admitting thirty-eight sworn enemies. No, there were really only thirty-seven. Walter Bronkowski loved me madly. I later found out that he actually belonged in the first grade. This would account for his lack of discrimination in the selection of love objects.

The pledge of allegiance was the only activity of the day which would go off with any degree of success. After that it was downhill all the way, and a rough trip it was.

To guard the secret of my inadequacies as a teacher, I kept the classroom doors and windows tightly closed, as if I expected a tornado at any minute. (As a matter of fact, I did.) In this way the riotous sounds could not escape to the other rooms. The lack of oxygen began to make us all slightly groggy by around three in the afternoon, but I found this condition a welcome change.

I restricted our physical education activities to a few indoor calisthenics, because I quickly learned that nowhere does a lack of control show up more clearly than on the playing field. Besides, the only game I knew was "Drop the Handkerchief," which my students scorned as a "first-grade game."

The end of the day always provided a fitting climax. Before the final bell, the children were supposed to place their chairs on top of the tables so that the custodian could sweep with a maximum of speed and ease. At 4:09 my words, "All right, boys and girls, put your chairs on your tables and line up," would produce an activity closely resembling a combination of the storming of the Bastille and the Russian bread riots.

When the last child was gone, I would wander despondently about the room for an hour, reliving the agonies of the day while I picked up the litter. I had to be sure to leave the room neat because custodians are notorious stool pigeons and are fast to inform the principal if "things don't look right."

Discipline and debris disposal, however, were only part of my trouble. I had even greater difficulty with teaching methods. Although the second-grade course-of-study manual outlined what I was required to teach, I had no idea how to teach it. For example, since my "slow learners" couldn't read at all, I decided to put them back into a beginning reading book. The first chapter was illustrated with several pictures of a tot in a ruffled dress holding a balloon. The heroine's emotions ran the gamut from delight, at the beginning, to anguish as the balloon escaped her and floated off into the sky. The entire text of the story was, "oh, oh; oh, oh, oh; oh, oh!" Now, how do you *teach* that to a circle of upturned, open-mouthed faces?

Then there were other baffling areas of instruction. The course of study directed me to teach the fundamentals of "manuscript," a form of printing with which I was unfamiliar. In arithmetic, I was supposed to impart, with concrete examples, the concepts of addition and subtraction. (That is, I couldn't just say, "Now memorize this: six and three are nine.") I was supposed to give the students music lessons in a room in which the only instrument available was an autoharp, which I couldn't play. My art instruction suffered because I didn't know how to keep the clay supply from turning to stone overnight or how to mix tempera paints so they wouldn't turn sour and attract flies. The school had a good educational film library, but I didn't know how to run a projector. I didn't know . . . but I could go on forever.

Why didn't the principal step in and either give me some tutoring or fire me? Well, it was her first semester as principal and she had troubles of her own. But probably the main reason I was allowed to go my inept way was that there was no one available to take my place, and while I was not better than anything else, I was better than nothing.

Then, just as I was ready to throw in the ruler in favor of a job clerking at Newberry's, the benevolent and protective Ford Foundation appeared on the scene. To alleviate the tense situation in the Los Angeles area, they set up a teacher training project at the University of Southern California. This program was designed to help people like me fulfill the requirements for a regular teaching credential by taking education courses on Saturdays and in the summer. I fell upon this opportunity like a thirsty second grader upon a drinking fountain.

It would be nice to be able to say that I found my thirty units of education courses thrilling and inspiring. Unfortunately, I didn't. Often, just as legend has it, they were dull and full of busy work. Nevertheless, I will admit, in classic educationese, that they were *meaningful* to me. As I learned something about methods, I was able to take hold in the classroom, my students began to learn what they were supposed to learn in the second grade, and I even found it possible to open the windows. Then, finally, as the screams of my nerves and conscience subsided, I started sleeping nights, and experiencing by day some of the feelings that make teachers stick to the profession.

My attitude now toward education courses can be summed up with a paraphrase of that old saying about money: "I have taught with education courses and without education courses, and, believe me, *with* is better." For just as an architect who wants to design a Guggenheim Museum must, in his college years, learn plumbing specifications, a teacher who wants to plant the kiss of the gods on the foreheads of his students has first to learn how to keep them sitting still long enough to make contact.

"Part of the American myth is that people who are handed the skin of a dead sheep at graduation time think it will keep their minds alive forever."

—JOHN MASON BROWN

The Process of Becoming

A college is often defined as an organized opportunity for self-education. A college president has stated that two-thirds of the students who graduate from college do so without getting an education. Obviously, one's education goes on all the time in both organized and unorganized situations. In other words, each of us is in the process of becoming. Then we must ask ourselves these questions: Becoming what? How can I be sure? Is that worth becoming? How do I deliberately, consciously pursue the process?

This unit is designed to structure your reading, thinking, and discussion around the problems and prospects inherent in the process of becoming. Applying an analysis of the process of becoming to yourself can be a most significant undertaking. Permitting oneself to become involved in self-understanding is a most difficult task, but it is the imperative element in the process of becoming.

Some Ideas for Discussion or Self-study

What are your reactions to this comment? "I believe I'll go into teaching because I just love children."

It has been stated by Harold Benjamin that each of us possesses certain socially useful idiosyncrasies and the responsibility of the school is to help us identify and nurture these rather than eliminate them. What is a socially useful idiosyncrasy? What socially useful idiosyncrasy do you possess? What is the nature of the school experience that develops your socially useful idiosyncrasy?

W. C. Fields rebelled at what he considered regimentation at school and he refused to attend. Do you regard this as a compliment to Fields? Is there any validity to his claim that the schools are too regimented? How is this regimentation an asset (or liability) to helping the individual "become"?

What is the nature of a school experience that contributes optimally to the "process of becoming"?

You have probably heard this comment made about a person:

"He is a born teacher." Is there any validity to this statement? How does a person become an outstanding teacher?

The "knowledge explosion" has forced an important rethinking of the educational process as applied to development of the individual. What are the implications for the individual personality?

So many adults have been heard to say: "I finished my education at . . ." This describes a common perception of what school is all about. What does such a statement imply relative to your own education? What is the significance of the statement for yourself as you utilize your college experience in the process of becoming?

About W. C. Fields, Who Said, "A Man Who Hates Dogs and Children Can't Be All Bad"

A Letter to a College of Education Faculty from Its Dean

I have just finished reading W. C. Fields, His Follies and His Fortunes* by Pulitzer-Prize winner Robert Lewis Taylor. As I was reading the book I felt I wanted to share something from it with you but what I did not know. I have already overdone writing about the moral that could be drawn from Fields' biography that the unschooled are often less inhibited and thus may have more originality than the schooled. I thought of writing about the perils of alcoholic beverages but Fields lived to be 67 years of age and worked constantly and that's pretty good in anybody's league, even if he finally did go out with a badly diseased liver. Some possible essay subjects built on Fields' career I thought about and discarded were: "The Culture as a Force in the Education of W. C. Fields," "School, Society and W. C. Fields," "The Value of Humor in the Teaching Process," and even "Humor Is Not Taught But Caught."

I had a strong desire to relate to you some incidents in Fields' life, such as the one that happened in the hospital, where Fields was domiciled for a time with a nervous condition that made his skin feel like one great sore. One morning a new nurse, for some reason, got mixed up and tried to pull a pillowcase, instead of the pajamas, over his sensitive feet. When the pillowcase would not come up the nurse tried to solve the problem by yanking it which caused Fields to sit up and give the nurse such an awful cursing that he was proud of this feat forever afterward. Later he declared, "When I did that I knew that I was going to get well."

I also wanted to tell you the anecdote about Fields and the rainmaker.

* Quotations in this article are taken from Robert Lewis Taylor, W. C. Fields, His Follies and His Fortunes, 1967, Signet Books.

Fields was a rain lover. Rain seemed to purge his mind of whatever torments had been assailing him. So when Fields was in Hollywood he had a problem because, as even people who live as far away from California as Florida know, Southern California is not famous for the quantity of its rainfall. In fact, Fields' biographer claims that many Californians lay bets that it is not likely to ever rain again in their place of abode. During his California stay Fields was therefore forced to the use of artificial rain. Once when Fields was at a spa recovering from an illness, he had his friend, Carlotta Monti, hook a garden hose to a handy tap and spray water on his cottage tin roof. Only with the water dropping on his roof could he go peacefully to sleep. A little later when Fields was able to go outside, Miss Monti rigged up a lawn umbrella, and while he rested beneath it she sat in a chair somewhat removed and pelted his retreat with the water from the hose. The biographer says, "It made an interesting sight for visitors to the spa—the famous comedian reading under his make-believe shower, the pretty Mexican near-by playing God."

Then there was another incident that concerned Field's conduct at a funeral which at first glance seemed to offer a moral upon which I could build something to write to you about. But I could never figure what the moral could be. This incident concerned the sad but interesting time spent by Fields' sporting group at John Barrymore's big funeral. On one side of the chapel sat the Barrymore family and certain elderly friends, "people long devoted to restrained behavior; on the other side were grouped the departed's rowdy companions including Fields. There was open evidence of hostility between the two factions. One was in favor of preserving the traditional solemnity of funerals, the other made its wishes known from time to time with statements like, 'Let's stop outside for a drink—Jack'd want it that way,' and 'We've got to carry on!' "

At the conclusion of the service, Gene Fowler, the author, was walking toward the mortician's limousine in which he had come to the funeral service.

"Don't be a sucker," hissed Fields, motioning with distaste toward the lugubrious black automobile. "Ride back in my car with me."

They got into the back seat of Fields' big Lincoln and the chauffeur drove slowly into the line of moving vehicles. When the procession had gone about a mile Fields directed the chauffeur to pull over to a vacant lot.

"What will you have to drink, a beer or martini?" Fields asked Fowler.

"Both," replied Fowler.

"A very wise decision," said Fields.

Fields made two double martinis (whatever that is) and opened two beers, then instructed the chauffeur to drive on. As they stopped for a red light, a couple of patrolmen in a prowl car, intent on enforcing the Los Angeles law against drinking in automobiles, pulled up beside them. Fields leaned out of a window and spoke to them sternly, "Sorry, my fine public servants, but I haven't enough of this nectar to pass about willy-nilly." To his chauffeur he shouted, "Drive on!" The policemen, confused, let them go.

After reading over again all of the above anecdotes I realized that there was no moral, respectable educational theme I could discover in any of them and therefore they were not fit to include in a letter to you. Also they did not give an expression of the dignity that my secretary requires of all material coming out of her office. So since I can recognize as well as the next fellow when defeat is staring me in the face I did not persist in trying to work these incidents in Fields' life into a letter to you. But as I still wanted to write to you about this book I thought of other ways to do it such as making a comparison or contrast between two largely self-educated persons; W. C. Fields, as depicted in this biography, and George Washington, as described in a biography by Douglas Southall Freeman, which I completed reading a few months ago. But my prudent side soon warned me that this was such a scandalous thought that I could not even allow my secretary to know I had thought it. (Incidentally, in case anyone might think that I am accusing someone else of prudishness I want to say here that I take sole responsibility for not putting W. C. Fields and George Washington in the same essay.)

In thinking about the personality of W. C. Fields I was reminded of a recent review of Walter Kerr's book, *Tragedy and Comedy*. This book by the noted *New York Times* drama critic began with the admission that he had not intended to write about tragedy; he wanted to write only about comedy. Kerr found that as he thought about comedy and explored its genesis that comedy could not be clearly discussed without continuous reference to tragedy. Comedy always followed tragedy. He concluded that laughter is not man's first impulse; he cries first. Then, in essence, comedy is composed of anguish and desire, and deals with their imperfect actuality. Kerr's theme seems to be following the lead given by Abraham Lincoln who said he laughed to keep from crying. Fields in this respect was like Lincoln, who, too, had a keen sense of humor but basically was an unhappy person. (Since unhappiness is so academically respectable I believe I have finally reached safe ground for an essay!)

Fields' life seemed to be dedicated to finding economic security for himself, to achieving the greatest possible expertness in juggling, and to pricking at pretentiousness, pomposity, and phoniness. In this last dedication, despite, or possible because of, the fact that he was himself often pretentious and pompous, he was able to depict these traits of character in a hilariously comical manner. Yet, paradoxically, Fields, who probably was one of the finest comedians who ever lived, did not find life very funny. Most of his humor seemed to be concerned with his intense desire to deflate the self-inflated whom he despised.

One of Fields' close acquaintances, after studying Fields for years, developed the theory that Fields' personal and professional life was dedicated to repaying society for the bruises and hurts he suffered during his childhood. "Nearly everything Bill tried to get into his movies was something that lashed out at the world," this acquaintance said. "The peculiar thing is that although he was being pretty mean there wasn't any real sting in it. It was only funny. Bill never really wanted to hurt anybody. He just felt an obligation."

Anyone who associated with Fields for very long had to contend with a great amount of bullying and minor fraud and to put up with his heavy martyrdom. Fields' biographer says that the movie censors "were obliged to keep an especially alert eye on Fields' bullying of children, both in the script and on set." Fields played in several films with the infant, Baby LeRoy, and he believed that the child was deliberately trying to wreck his career. The comedian knew that people would watch the baby instead of him in a scene if all things were equal, so he made a special effort to see to it that they were not equal. He worked as hard to steal scenes away from the baby as if he were an adult. Between the filming Fields sat in a corner, eyeing the child while muttering vague but terrible sounding threats. Once when action was suspended so that the child could have his orange juice, Fields asked the infant's nurse to take a breather while he gave "the little nipper his juice." The nurse nodded gratefully and left the set. Immediately Fields "strengthened the citrus with a generous noggin of gin." When the shooting was ready to recommence, Baby LeRoy was "in a state of inoperative bliss." Yet while Fields was actually jealous of the child, he would give him presents and make "sheepish and comradely gestures on the sly." One time when the child actor's option was due, Fields, in an attempt to emphasize Baby LeRoy's importance to the studio, wrote a part for the baby in his picture. In his home Fields had a photograph, prominently displayed, of himself and Baby LeRoy together riding kiddie cars. Yet Fields usually gave the snarling reply when an interviewer asked how he liked children, "Fried," or "Parboiled," or something worse.

Eric Hoffer has shown in his *True Believer* how typically the suppressed become the oppressors when they get on top. This was to a degree true with Fields. He had been forced to suffer terribly by adults when he was a child and as an adult instead of wanting to show compassion and demonstrate love toward children he believed his role should be just the opposite. When he did show compassion and love he tried to hide it. Fields somehow equated compassion and love with phoniness. He believed that he had learned from life that the emotions that serve one best are tough emotions. (Fields had some of the virtues that are needed by a dean of a poor, struggling little college with no academic reputation. Fields would have had the patrons of the college believing that Harvard was in second place to his institution in academic standards.)

Fields' outwardly expressed philosophy toward people was given in his last film "Never Give a Sucker an Even Break," which he wrote under his pen name of Otis Criblecoblis. The title of the film was not just a joke with Fields. For him it was a commandment to be strictly followed. Fields in his life had taken on his father, dogs, children, policemen, alligators, trains, church deacons, swans, servants, movie magnates and waiters and had almost always been the loser, except with movie magnates, and therefore he did not dare give his opposition an even break. His failures and tribulations had given him "a vast watchful suspicion of society and its patterns." This uneasiness shaped his art. In "The Bank Dick," for instance, when he became upset upon seeing a teller in a straw hat he was only reenacting an actual experience of opening his first bank account after a brief conversation with the president. As Fields was leaving the bank he remembered that the president had his hat on at his desk. This worried Fields for years. He kept checking back to see if the president kept his hat on at his desk because he was ready to run off with all of the funds of the bank.

The biographer of W. C. Fields, His Follies and Fortunes, says that Fields "as a national comic phenomenon had no counterpart." He says that while the applied skill of Chaplin and other comedians delighted audiences, followers of funny men laughed at the mention of Fields' name. Taylor writes:

> Sensing this curious state of the public's mind, William Le Baron, former head of production at Paramount, for whom Fields made some of his best movies, conceived the idea of opening movies of the master by showing only his feet walking. There was nothing especially hilarious about Field's feet, though a full rear view of him, with all its pomp and fraudulent dignity, was uproarious. Without exception, however, audiences responded with noisy appreciation to their truncated first glimpse of the star.
>
> One of Fields' friends once said that this spontaneous merriment was due to the popular notion of his personal life. Fields' defiance of civilization, over a period of sixty-seven years, became an institution in

which the public took pride. His work was indistinguishable from his life; when people applauded Fields' feet they were cheering his escape from the humdrum.

Despite our concerns these days with big brother, mass education, alienations, academic respectability, grades, realities, illusions, automation, urban blight, poverty, the administration, courses of study, crime, Republicans, Democrats, marchers, hippies, squares, teen-agers, drouths, hurricanes, Viet Nam, status symbols, revolts, organizational charts, deans, chairmen of the boards, committees, what's "in," hemlines, culture, and life, it may not hurt us to pause, without having to give any educational excuse, long enough to laugh with W. C. Fields.

Gene Buck, once the principal assistant to Florenz Zeigfeld, who picked Fields out of vaudeville in 1914 and hired him for the Follies, wrote of the comedian in a letter to a friend soon after Fields' death:

> He was amazing and unique, the strangest guy I ever knew in my lifetime. He was all by himself. Nobody could be like him and a great many tried. He was so damn different, original and talented. He never was a happy guy. He couldn't be, but what color and daring in this game of life! He made up a lot of new rules forty years ago about everything: conduct, people, morals, entertainment, friendship, gals, pals, fate and happiness, and he had the courage to ignore old rules.
>
> When I first met him he had taken a terrible kicking around in life, and he was tough, bitter and cynical in an odd, humorous way. He was as good then as he was at his peak. His gifts and talents as an entertainer and comic were born in him, I think. Some guys learn through experience and practice being comics. Not Bill. God made him funny. . . . I've had a lot to do with comics and their development and assisted and transplanted many of them during my humble course, and I just want to say that when Bill left the other day, something great in the world died, and something very badly needed."

With no further comment on the follies, foibles, and fortunes of W. C. Fields, I close.

New Ways to Actualize
Our Potential

Suggestions on how man can make more effective use of his higher
mental powers for his own benefit and the good of society must start
with a searching appraisal of the present, free from ancient shibboleths.
Any society that accepts the view that it has reached near perfection
impedes its own progress. The first problem, then, is to look objectively
at the present state of Western civilization from the vantage point of
man's entire history. How much progress has been made? How well has
Western society solved its problems? How much better is it than the
civilizations that have gone before?

One thing is certain. Civilization does not proceed at a regular pace
and in a straight line. There are great plateaus where no progress is ap-
parent—in fact, periods when civilization seems to have slipped backward. Then, with little advance indication, comes a strong upward thrust.

Progress is often confined to a single area. It is debatable whether
present-day Western civilization is on a plateau in most respects, despite
great progress in one special area—that of science. Certainly a good case
can be made that modern man does not use his intellectual powers to
any greater extent than did the citizen of ancient Greece. He enjoys far
more wealth and comfort and greater freedom from disease, yet modern
man shows no evidence of being able to manage his own life with greater
intelligence than did his ancient forebears. Nor does he solve the problems that face society in his day with markedly greater skill than earlier
generations.

These observations relate to Western man. It is easy to forget that
there are still many people inhabiting the earth today who have not
reached the level of Neolithic man. Only a minority of the three billion
human beings alive today could claim to have reached as high a cultural
plane as that of the Greco-Roman era.

George Gallup, *The Miracle Ahead*, New York, Harper & Row, copyright © 1964
by George Gallup, pp. 23–25, 199–204. Reprinted by permission of Harper & Row,
Publishers.

Many of the observations and proposals made in the pages that follow concern the general state of mankind. Others deal particularly with the United States and its special problems and are not applicable, therefore, to all nations—not even to those making up the group described as the West.

Our special concern is how civilization can be lifted to a new level. To accomplish this feat, suggestions have been grouped into four main categories, each of which will be dealt with at some length. A brief summary of the categories follows.

The first has to do with individual effort. A new educational philosophy is required—a plan that embraces the entire life span of the individual and which, in the earlier years, places major emphasis upon learning to use the mind as opposed to the mere memorizing of facts. In view of the "explosion of knowledge" which has taken place largely within the last three decades, one of the necessary functions of schooling must be to teach students to distinguish between the important and the unimportant. The new philosophy of education must take account of teaching machines, with the teacher freed to devote more thought to the greatest of all educational tasks—how to create and maintain the excitement inherent in the learning process.

The second category of suggestions deals with the great opportunities that can be capitalized upon through collective effort. Up to this point in history mankind has failed to make effective use of the talents of the great mass of people. In the United States, and presumably in many other nations, hundreds of millions of man-hours of mental effort go to waste each year because no serious effort has ever been made to use the collective brain power in the solution of problems at all levels—local, state, and national. Elected officials, congressional committees, and scientific groups have foundered in trying to solve many of the nation's more persistent problems, largely because they have not organized the conditions under which effective solutions can be produced. There is one notable exception. At least one great achievement of recent years, which will be described later, indicates how man working in concert with his fellow men can achieve wonders when conditions are properly ordered.

The third category deals with the opportunities made possible by new scientific procedures. The present scientific era was ushered in by the application of empirical methods, strongly advocated by Francis Bacon early in the seventeenth century. Methodology largely accounts for the amazing progress of physical science in the years since. New procedures are now available for use in the realm of social science—methods that are as promising for the solution or amelioration of social problems as the methods of Bacon were for problems of the natural world. The development of the electronic computer opens a whole new area of research and provides the chance to find the reasons why certain practices and institutions fail while others succeed.

The fourth category has to do with the problem of change. The goals that any society recognizes are largely constant over long periods of time. The means to achieve these goals must change as knowledge and experience accumulate and as conditions of life change. Since change is vital to a growing culture, it is important to examine all of the various resistances to change and to develop ways of overcoming these resistances. Society itself must accept most of the blame for the failure of social institutions and practices to keep abreast of new conditions of life brought about by progress in physical science. There is much evidence to prove that resistance to change is not inherent in man, and the great hope of the future is that a new point of view can be established toward the necessity for change in social and political forms and practices. In the whole history of man no single generation has been taught to understand change and to seek change. The educational program must accept this responsibility, not only to break the shackles of the past but to contribute to the mental health and advancement of the oncoming generations.

Preparing for Change

Even though resistance to change springs from many sources, it is possible to overcome it in some instances, modify it in others. The fact that Western man actually courts change in some areas of life provides evidence that resistance to change is not inherent in his thinking. There is the further comforting thought: *In the whole history of man, no generation has been taught to expect change, to be prepared for change, or to seek change.*

The importance of preparing the individual for change has never been fully understood; nor has the importance of change in the advancement of society been fully recognized. If each new generation is to be indoctrinated with its importance, then the reasons for change must be more fully appreciated.

One of the most cogent reasons for accepting change concerns the mental health of the individual. In a highly complex society with its many anxiety-inducing factors, mental illness often results from the inability to adapt readily to new situations. On the other hand, proof that acceptance of change contributes to mental health—and to long life—

has already been offered. The centenarians and nonagenarians investigated displayed a remarkable ability to accept chang ewithout mental disturbance. They took change in their stride.

The importance of being prepared for change can be illustrated by three situations arising during periods of war. The first example comes from World War II and has to do with the calm and collected manner in which the residents of London and other cities of Great Britain endured the bombings to which they were subjected almost nightly. Residents of these cities amazed the world by refusing to become nervous wrecks as a result of these daily brushes with death. They had prepared themselves for such an ordeal, and had adjusted their lives and their thinking accordingly.

In another war situation, lack of this mental resiliency and adaptability ended in disaster. The American soldiers who were taken prisoner by the Communists in the Korean War were unprepared for what might happen to them in the event that they fell into the hands of the enemy and were subjected to many kinds of torment, physical and mental. They had not been conditioned to meet such a situation; and as a result, many literally crumbled mentally and physically and died in shocking numbers. It was not their special weakness that brought about this collapse; other Americans of their age would have fallen apart as rapidly. It was the lack of proper instruction. They had not been conditioned to accept change.

By way of contrast, the Jews who were sent to Nazi concentration camps had steeled themselves to the awful horrors that they knew, or suspected, were in store for them. They gave a remarkable demonstration of how man can adjust to even the most cruel and inhuman torture when he is mentally prepared.

Since mental health has an important bearing upon physical health, conditioning the individual to embrace change is reason enough for making an effort to orient each new generation to expect and to welcome it. Even more important, only through change of a drastic order will man begin to actualize his potentialities. The opportunities that lie ahead in the fuller employment of brain power cannot be realized if man chains himself to the *status quo*.

The driving force for change and for making better use of man's mental abilities must come from the public, not from its leaders. This may seem unusual, until it is recognized that much of the opposition to change comes from the very persons who might be expected to advocate it most vigorously.

The field of education offers a good example. If major changes are to take place in the educational system, the movement is not likely to be led by educators. Persons who have struggled through a long period of training in a particular field and who have subsequently established themselves in positions of leadership cannot be expected to fight very hard for changing the system, no matter what its shortcomings. Educators are not alone in this failing. The same principle applies to militarists, journalists, businessmen, diplomats, doctors, lawyers, politicians, and those engaged in any profession or calling where much training is required and positions of authority and leadership are hard to achieve.

The penalties for instituting—or even advocating—change can be severe. Leaders risk their positions of leadership. Moreover, change of any kind requires a certain amount of readjustment, and if the change is great, it can require much time and effort spent in relearning. The leader who advocates radical change is almost certain to incur the wrath of other leaders in his field, and of the rank and file as well. Witness the educators, militarists, and medical practitioners who have fought for important and needed changes in their fields, only to reap a harvest of scorn from their co-workers.

Society must recognize that as a result of these pressures, change cannot be brought about easily by its leaders, except in those situations in which the changes advocated do not disturb present relationships. In fact, it is the leaders who typically become the most bitter and the most effective foes of change. The public, therefore, must take the initiative and assume responsibility for progress in the affairs of man. *The public must force change upon its leaders.*

Unfortunately, the public cannot look to experts or specialists, for the very same reasons that it cannot expect change to be initiated by its leaders. With the trend toward greater specialization, the expert and specialist command more respect today than they perhaps deserve. The expert merits respect for his sepcial knowledge; but like the leader, he is expert in his small world as it presently exists, not expert in the world as it might be. Although he plays an important role in modern society, it is not realistic to expect him to advocate drastic change. This is the surest way for him to lose his status of expert.

Any intrusion into these special fields by laymen is likely to be resented by expert and leader alike. For this reason, the layman must be prepared to accept abuse and ridicule. The expert will do everything he can to keep the layman at a distance. One stratagem has been found effective in countering any new idea offered by an outsider. Henry George described it this way: "The first thing they say is that it isn't true. And when its truth can no longer be denied, they say it isn't important. And when its importance is firmly established, they say it isn't new."

The hope of the future rests with the citizen. To be effective, he must be well informed, and he must discover ways of making better use of his own great mental capacities and those of his fellow men. He cannot expect his leaders to give him much help in his upward march. Woodrow Wilson expressed the thought this way when he said, "The great struggling unknown masses . . . are the dynamic force that is lifting the levels of society. A nation is as great, and only as great, as her rank and file."

Conclusion

Can man perform the miracle of lifting himself to a higher level of civilization?

The answer is Yes—unequivocally. Man is clearly in charge of his own evolution; he can proceed at a pace that he himself sets.

He can solve any problem that comes within his purview—even the problem of war. The great advances made in physical science can be paralleled in social science. Man now has the procedures for dealing with the problems arising out of his social existence—problems that the methods of physical science cannot adequately explore or illuminate.

Man has scarcely begun to make use of his almost limitless brain power, either individually or collectively. Lack of progress in dealing with the affairs of mankind can be traced to a simple truth; man has never made a concerted and persistent effort to solve his social and political problems. His inventive genius has been confined almost exclusively to the production of better tools and instruments.

The next great move forward can now be taken. All that is required is a firm belief in man's great potentialities and a readiness to accept change.

Man is still young on the face of the earth; civilization is still in its infancy. *Homo sapiens* has not yet realized his strength and his greatness; nor does he see, except dimly, the heights to which civilization can reach.

Three hundred years ago it was equally difficult to foresee the great advances in science that the future held in store. Only Francis Bacon had that vision. He also had a vision of man with which this book might properly close: "Men are not animals erect but immortal gods."

ROBERT L. SHANNON

Are You Doing What You Should or What You Could?

"Poor old Temple—spent his life doing what he should, instead of what he could." In a conversation with himself, Temple offers this projection of what he expects people to say about him if he continues his present way of living. About twenty years of age, Temple is the grandson of Benjamin Franklin in the recent Broadway musical, "Ben Franklin in Paris." Temple behaves as the obedient, conscientious grandson. He carries out Ben Franklin's ideas and proposals with preciseness and accurateness. Temple is dependable, predictable, reliable, and thorough. This grandson implements the ideas of grandfather, and he does it flawlessly. But, Temple never behaves as an innovative, imaginative, socially secure idea man in his own right. His potential for self and society is dormant.

The behavior of Temple is amazingly similar to that of many college students I met. It is equally prevalent among many experienced teachers. These students and teachers choose to dedicate their college years to "doing what they should." They by-pass the intense excitement, satisfaction, and personal emergence that comes from "doing what they could."

Today's college students are terrific. Those who are teacher candidates are, for the most part, potentially sensational. In too many instances these splendid prospects for teaching expend their energies and intellects figuring out plausible justifications to themselves for going through a program of teacher preparation by collecting courses, grades, and credits. Obligations are met, teaching recipes are copied down, meaningless phrases are memorized, courses are passed, and degrees are acquired by whole populations of prospective teachers who elect to "do what they should—instead of what they could."

The shift to "doing what you could" does not mean growing a beard, cutting classes, rejecting religion, or staying awake all night. Such behavior is like joining a lodge where every member follows the approved code of living. "Doing what you could" is to become a vital participant in the world of ideas.

In his book *Reminiscences*, General Douglas MacArthur wrote: "The

177

one thing in the world that cannot be stopped is a sound idea. The individual may be martyred, but his thoughts live on."

It seems to be generally accepted that education includes a pursuit of truth. Pursuit of truth cannot mean smooth repetition of a college professor's conceptions of truth. It must insist on an active, personal involvement of the student in the world of ideas. There must never be a day in the life of the prospective teacher when he fails to have an idea and try out his idea in the university setting. Pursuit of truth by way of the world of ideas must begin with a truthful and positive conception of self as a person with ideas. Such a conception is nurtured to appropriate fulfillment when the teacher candidate is "doing what he could—instead of what he should."

HAROLD BENJAMIN

The Cultivation of Idiosyncrasy

Harold Benjamin has for years delighted audiences and readers with his penetrating yet gentle satires on some of our traditional beliefs and practices in education. In this article, he presents an amusing allegory with the underlying purpose of challenging the tendency toward uniformity in public education and calling for the cultivation of every socially useful idiosyncracy.

In a tale given to American educators by George H. Reavis, the wild creatures once had a school in the woods. All the animals had to take all the subjects. Swimming, running, jumping, climbing, and flying made up the required curriculum.

This was a school of no nonsense. It was a good, liberal educational institution. It gave broad general training—and instruction—and education, too.

Some animals, of course, were better students than others. The squirrel, for example, got straight A's from the first in running, jumping, and climbing. He got a good passing grade, moreover, in swimming. It looked as though he would make Phi Beta Kappa in his junior year, but he had trouble with flying. Not that he was unable to fly. He could fly. He climbed to the top of tree after tree and sailed through the air to neighboring trees with ease. As he modestly observed, he was a flying squirrel by race. The teacher of flying pointed out, however, that he should take off in the approved fashion from the ground. Indeed, the teacher decided that the taking-off-from-the-ground unit had to be mastered first, as was logical, and so he drilled the squirrel day after day on the take-off.

The flying teacher's practice in this case was in strict accord with the educational philosophy of the school. The teachers recognized that students would necessarily display great variations in their abilities. In the

Harold Benjamin, *The Cultivation of Idiosyncrasy*, The Inglis Lecture, Cambridge, Mass., Harvard University Press, copyright 1949 by the President and Fellows of Harvard College. Reprinted 1949. by permission of Harvard University Press.

Woods Normal School, as a matter of fact, the teachers had learned a great deal about individual differences and the consequent tremendous ranges in human capacities. They set themselves doggedly, therefore, to the task of reducing these differences as best they might, that sane likenesses, safe unities, and noble conformities might prevail in the woods.

The squirrel tried hard. He tried so hard he got severe Charley horses in both hind legs, and thus crippled he became incapable even of running, jumping, or climbing. He left school a failure, and died soon thereafter of starvation, being unable to gather and store nuts. He was cheerful to the last and was much beloved by his teachers and fellow pupils. He had the highest regard for his alma mater, regretting only the peculiar incapacity which had kept him from passing the course in flying.

The snake was a promising student also. Being a combination tree-and-water snake, he was excellent in both climbing and swimming. He was also a superior runner and passed the tests in that subject with ease. But he began to show antisocial tendencies in arguments with the instructor in jumping. When he had been given the basic instruction in that subject and it came time for him to make his first jump, he coiled up and threw himself almost his full length. This was not jumping, said the teacher. It was merely striking—a snake skill—and not at all the general-education jumping which all cultivated creatures had to know.

The teacher of jumping remonstrated with him, tried to get him to jump properly, and used the very best methods taught in the more advanced demonstration schools, but the snake became more and more uncooperative. The school counselors and the principal were called in and decided to attempt to vary the snake's education by teaching him flying but to their distress he flatly refused even to attend the preliminary classes in that subject. He did not say he was unable to fly—he merely scoffed at the notion of flying for a snake and said he had no intention of ever bothering with the subject. The more the teachers argued with him the more he coiled and struck and sneered, and the more he sneered and coiled and struck the more bitter and introverted he became. He left school and made his living briefly as a highwayman, murdering other animals along the woods path, until he struck at a wildcat one evening and was clawed to death for his lack of judgment. He died detested by all and mourned by none.

The eagle was a truly brilliant student. His flying was superb, his running and jumping were of the best, and he even passed the swimming test, although the teacher tried to keep him from using his wings too much. By employing his talons and beak, moreover, he could climb after a fashion and no doubt he would have been able to pass that course, too, except that he always flew to the top of the problem tree or cliff when the teacher's back was turned and sat there lazily in the sun, preening his feathers and staring arrogantly down at his fellow students, climbing up the hard way. The teachers reasoned with him to no avail. He would not study climbing seriously. At first he turned aside the faculty's importunities with relatively mild wisecracks and innuendoes, but as the teachers put more pressure upon him he reacted with more and more feeling. He became very aggressive, stating harshly and boldly that he knew more about climbing than did the professor of that subject. He became very successful when he left school and he attained high position in the woods society. He was dogmatic and dictatorial, respected by all and feared by many. He became a great supporter of general education. He wanted the curriculum of his alma mater to remain just as it was, except that he believed climbing had no general cultural value and should be replaced by some more liberal subject, like dive-bombing, which in his view, gave the student a certain general polish superior even to that given by the study of flying.

The gopher parents thought that the school was very good in most matters and that all the subjects had excellent results if properly taught, but they wanted their children to learn digging in addition to the general education. The teachers regarded digging as a manual skill not elevated enough for general culture. Besides, they did not know how to dig and they resisted learning such a subject.

So the gophers withdrew their children from this institution and hired a practical prairie dog to set up a private school in which an extensive course was given in digging. The prairie-dog schoolmaster also taught courses in running, jumping, swimming, and climbing. He did not teach flying. He said it was an outmoded subject. Digging, a more practical subject, took its place in the curriculum. So the ducks and geese and wild turkeys and prairie chickens all scoffed at the prairie-dog's school. They set up schools of their own, very much like the others schools except that the ducks and geese emphasized diving and the wild turkeys and prairie chickens gave advanced courses in evasive air tactics.

At this juncture, Old Man Coyote, who had been studying the development of education in the woods, shrewdly observed, "All these pedagogical characters are going at this business wrong-end-to. They look at what animals and birds—a lot of animals and birds—do and need to do. Then they put those needs and those doings into formal schoolings and try to make the little pups and cubs and fledglings fit the schoolings. It's haywire, wacky, and will never really work right."

Tom Gunn's Mule, a sour-visaged individual ready to criticize all theories, heard Old Man Coyote's remark and demanded harshly, "If you're so smart, how would you do it?"

"Why, I would turn the whole thing around," explained Old Man Coyote modestly.

"Turn it around?" scoffed Tom Gunn's Mule. "What d'ye mean, turn it around?"

"These school people start with things that the birds and animals do —or even more often what they did some time ago," explained Old Man Coyote. "There the teachers hammer these doings—or as much of them as they can handle and as they think high-toned enough—into schoolings, courses, curriculums, and subjects. Then they hammer the pups into the schoolings. It's a rough and dopey process, and the teachers have had to invent good explanations to defend it. Discipline, culture, systematic training—things like that—are what the teachers use for this purpose. I don't know what they mean and I think the teachers don't know what they mean, but I do know they make a lot of cubs and pups and fledglings mean and rough and dopey when they could and should make them good and slick and smart."

"Sure, sure," snorted Tom Gunn's Mule, "but you still haven't told me how you would do it."

"Turn it around," said Old Man Coyote. "Start with the pups. See what the pups do. Then see what the school can do for the pups. Then see what the pups and the school together can do for all the creatures in the woods. Simple—forwards instead of backwards—right-end-to instead of wrong-end-to."

Old Man Coyote turned triumphantly and started to trot away.

"Hey!" shouted Tom Gunn's Mule. "Wait!" These teachers have schools now. They have to run those schools. They are practical people. Just how specifically and precisely, would you tell them to change their schools so as to get their education right-end-to, as you call it?"

Old Man Coyote patted a yawn with the back of his forepaw. "I lay down general principles," he said. "These school teachers have got to figure out some of the minor details themselves."

This is the end of the story, but I am a school teacher myself, and so I have been trying to figure out a few of the details upon which Old Man Coyote touched. . . .

. . . I believe that the central question . . . is one which a democratic society may ignore only at its deadly peril.

The question is double-barrelled:

1. How much uniformity does this society need for safety?
2. How much deviation does this society require for progress?

The insight with which the line of safety is drawn and the skill with which the conditions of progress are embodied in an educational program determines in large measure whether a particular society will be a great society or a mean society, whether it will be strong or weak, whether it will be enduring or evanescent, whether it will be a creator and bearer of high meanings or a purveyor of the insignificances of ignorance and brutality.

The first steps in determining an educational program, whether for an entire national group, for a particular profession, or for a small number of students in a classroom, are the steps that are most commonly slighted. They are often assumed to have been taken when in fact they have been by-passed.

What are these first steps? Let us look at an example. Because the defenders of educational plainsmanship are often especially worried over a lack of the uniformities which they consider necessary for national security, let us take our first example from the area of military education. . . .

"Whenever I met one of them generals who fit by note," said Nathan Bedford Forrest accurately and without false modesty, "I always whipped him before he could pitch the tune." If Forrest could have been sent to West Point in his youth and trained into being a more faithful copy of Braxton Bragg or Samuel. D. Sturgis, if General George Washington had been commissioned in the British Regulars at an early age and made much more like Lord Howe or Charles Lee, if Chief Joseph of the Nez Percés and Crazy Horse of the Oglala Sioux could only have had the advantages of a military education to model them after Captain Fetterman and Colonel Custer, the history of the United States' wars would be considerably less marked by peaks.

It is an ironic testimonial to the power of the *educational plainsman's philosophy* that in the very field of human endeavor where cultivated idiosyncrasy pays off most spectacularly and in clearest-cut physical terms, the doctrine of the approved doctrine, the uniformity of the uniform practice, and the massing of mediocrity should have held such undisputed sway. Here if anywhere it might perhaps seem that educators would revolt against the practices of pedagogical plainsmanship and become educational mountaineers. Here was where mountaineering would give results which nations commonly assess at high value. But the strength of conformity-enforcing agencies was too great. The shadow of Frederick of Prussia with his stiffly aligned peasants-in-arms moving in unison was too much even for men who saw demonstrated almost every year the battle superiority in American woods of non-alignment and non-unison. No matter; the principle of the pedagogical plainsman still triumphed. It was never more brilliantly expressed in action than on that memorable day on the Monongahela when Major General Sir Edward Braddock lined up his exhausted men as they staggered from the woods and gave a stiff dose of manual-of-arms and close-order drill in preparation for the coming attack of the French and Indian skirmishers. Almost two centuries later, his spiritual and professional descendants still keep his memory green by an improved manual-of-arms and an improved close-order drill which are just as effective today as their predecessors were in the middle of the eighteenth century.

We still educate second lieutenants by a combination of the concepts of noble-traits and uniform specific skills. How else can we train them? Is not war a demander of standardized routines, of interchangeable parts. We dress soldiers alike; why should we not educate them alike? . . .

Would you then not have a standard education for infantry officers? Would there be no minimum essentials for second lieutenants? Gad, Sir! I can see the veins turn purple in the colonel's neck. I can hear his fist hammer on the desk.

But not all colonels would so respond—not nearly so many as you might think; not even so many colonels, perhaps, as presidents and chancellors, deans and professors, superintendents and principals, teachers and headmasters, regents and trustees, parents and clergymen, legislators and those men-in-the-street who sometimes return to their homes and write letters to the editor.

All of us tend to echo these doubting cries. All of us are prisoners of our schooling—a schooling based on some combination of the concepts of the uniform and level noble traits or specific skills. The first article on our pedagogical faith is the *credo* of minimum standards. That *credo* lies flatly athwart the law and the gospel of Old Man Coyote's theory of education.

Old Man Coyote insists that the boy whose mathematical, linguistic, geographical, or other peaks of ability are built to great heights will have his valleys of ability in other areas pulled up towards his peaks until the sum of his achievements will be far above the minimum essentials ever set by plodding plainsman. Old Man Coyote insists further that the learner must go above his present peaks and valleys as a free, daring, and enterprising individual and never as one herded under the lash of a minimum standard.

This is a hard doctrine for us to accept. It is hard for us because we have confused our minimum standards with our objectives.

Our objective, in the case of military education, for example, is to keep the peace as long as possible and when wars break out, to stop them as quickly and efficiently as we can. The minimum essential is a lazy plainsman's device for shortcutting the objective. The sturdy mountaineer looks keenly across the land at the goal as he ascends every peak.

The observed facts of human development support Old Man Coyote's doctrine. Few if any men ever become great historians or great citizens by studying the outlines of history required in the freshman year. Few if any men ever become great infantry leaders by concentrating on the dead level of infantry fundamentals. Few if any great jurists, painters, industrialists, or musicians ever attained their heights of uniqueness by drill on the minimum essentials.

"But, Gad, Sir!" repeats my hypothetical colonel or professor or Tom Gunn's Mule, "We are not educating great generals, unusual soldiers, geniuses—we are just aiming modestly and in a common-sense way to train ordinary, dead-level, good infantry officers—interchangeable-stand-ard-uniform. You'd have them know how to load and fire an M-1, wouldn't you?"

"Ah!" says Old Man Coyote, "I would have no ordinary, dead-level officers—they would all be great officers in terms of their abilities—because that's a better way to win wars—and certainly some of them might not speak English or know how to load and fire an M-1 rifle. Some of them might speak only Spanish, for instance, in the San Martin Corps of the United States Foreign Legion, and some of them might command only mortar platoons."

"A likely situation," snorts Tom Gunn's Mule.

"It would be a lot more likely in the American Army," softly observes Old Man Coyote, "if the present brass had been educated forwards instead of backwards."

I have used these second lieutenants as examples in part because the objective of their education is relatively easy to see. Let us now consider examples of a kind of education which perhaps does not have such easily seen objectives.

Suppose it is teachers rather than infantry officers whom we are educating. Suppose we need one thousand new teachers in Massachusetts or Maryland next fall. Shall we seek in the teachers' colleges of these states to turn out a thousand more or less faithful copies of a model teacher? Shall we give marks of A to those more nearly approaching the approved pattern and marks of C and D to those furthest away from the pattern but still not so far away as to deserve being failed? Do we really want them all to act, look, talk, teach, and think alike? Are the deviations from the model which they display merely the measures of our inefficiency in teaching them, in bringing them up to the straight-A standards of near perfection.

"Ah! No, no!" we say hastily. "We who educate teachers have studied individual differences. Most of us who are old enough to affect the policies of teaching-training institutions studied individual differences in Volume III of Edward L. Thorndike's *Educational Psychology*, first published in 1914. We have known about individual differences for a long, long time. We try to develop the individual differences, the idiosyncrasies, of these teachers. We want to develop their idiosyncrasies in groups. We want blocks of idiosyncrasy. We need fifty different kinds of teachers next year, English and Social Studies teachers for small high schools, boys' physical education teachers who can also take a section in biology, mathematics and physics teachers, girls' counselors who can teach French, vocational agriculture teachers, home economics teachers, and so on. Certainly we want idiosyncrasies—in standard groups, that is."

The Old Man Coyote murmurs that we want developed useful idiosyncrasies. Useful for what? Useful for our objectives?

Are those objectives standard, minimum-essential objectives? They should not be. They should be as varied as the children whose learning these teachers are to aid.

We want one thousand uniquely educated teachers. We want teachers whose idiosyncrasies have been nurtured for unique learnings in schools.

Here is a prospective teacher whose interests and abilities in the nature and processes of child growth and development are exceptional. We shall not try to hold him back in this idiosyncrasy in order to flatten his ability peaks. We shall work with him to build up those peaks.

Shall we then ignore this prospective teacher's valleys of ability in written communication, in science, or in mathematics? Not at all, but we shall try to haul them up only by tying them to his rising peaks of ability. If we build his peak of understanding and skill in child growth and development high enough, his lower abilities in speaking, writing, computing, and biology can be brought far above the modest levels set by a plainsman's minimum essentials. . . .

Questions like these provide the real test of adherence to a theory of education as the cultivation of idiosyncrasy. The educational mountaineer replies to them by saying that no subject is pedagogically sacred, no matter what its patriotic, religious, or utilitarian status may be; that only the individual personality is an end in itself, and that education must therefore be a process of developing individuals by means of schoolings rather than a process of bringing learners up to a standard of schoolings.

The plainsman does not often say just the opposite of this, but he has to act thus or betray his plainsmanship. He is forced into a series of acts which constitute much of the business of many modern systems of education.

There is first and always the business of curriculum construction. In general education, it is a process not only of determining what is a sacred subject but also of assessing degrees of sacredness and indicating where in a child's life the subject should be learned. Thus the Gettysburg Address is obviously sacred and must be memorized by all sixth graders. What is the verdict on Washington's Farewell Address? It is not quite so sacred perhaps and does not need to be memorized. Let it be studied by all ninth graders carefully and respectfully. What of Franklin's Autobiography? Of Hamilton's and Madison's essays? Of Grant's Memoirs? Of Franklin D. Roosevelt's speeches?

If Cervantes is to be studied by everyone in high school, where are Goethe, Dante, and Racine to be met? If the multiplication tables to twelve are needed by everybody fourteen years of age, twelve times thirteen, fifteen times nineteen, and many other combinations as far as twenty times twenty must be good general education for many if not all persons who are eighteen years of age.

This is the first mark of the pedagogical plainsman, therefore; that he is continually constructing curricula, sorting subjects, fussing over facts, determining the significance of dates, tampering with time allotments, and computing percentages of sacredness.

He can be seen most clearly when he is working on very simple materials.

"Ah, 1492," he mutters, "there's a must for Americans and 1776—no doubt about that one—it goes in the *all-100 percent* compartment; so do 1812, 1898, 1917, and 1941. Those are easy, but some of these others are difficult; 1789, 1848, 1912, and 1933, for example; 1789 can't be quite so sacred—it is French and hence foreign—put it in high school European history where it is not required; and 1933 is college stuff and not really a foundation of Americanism—it is New Dealish besides."

The most popular exemplification of the pedagogical plainsman's curriculum theory is found in the ratio quiz program; its most high-toned manifestation is in current lists of great books. It was never more dramatically displayed in action on this continent than when the Ghost Dance craze swept over the Western country in the eighties of the last century. Here was a sacred schooling for a defeated, starving people. The Indians must dance, the ghostly teachers said, and Tauka Wakan would then wipe out the white men and bring back the buffalo. There was just one subject—the sacred dance. It made its graduates immune to white man's weapons. It was the greatest single educational short cut ever offered to Americans but its vogue ended abruptly on December 24, 1889, as a battery of four Hotchkiss guns poured explosive shells into a huddled group of Indian men, women, and children.

The quiz-program masters are just playing at education for a sheltered people's escapism, and thus they have need for only play counters in their game. The great-books professors have a closed game, very serious, and, since they pay all bets in great-books chips, they can operate happily so long as they stay inside the charmed circle. The unfortunate Sioux ghost-dancers at Wounded Knee Creek were forced to count their scores with their lives; their subject was not sacred enough for Hotchkiss guns.

A corollary activity for the pedagogical plainsman is the drawing of curricular distinctions. He traces the boundaries between general education and special education, between liberal studies and special education, between liberal studies and vocational training, between pure science and applied science, between the arts and the humanities, betwen philosophy and religion, between psychology and sociology, between history and anthropology, and so on and on into the academic night.

The more boundaries he surveys, the more new ones he discovers. He finds subjects within subjects, heaps classifications upon dichotomies, and uncovers new fields for education in never-ending labor.

In the plainsman's practice, the duty of the individual learner is clear. He must acquire, adjust, and conform. He must acquire subjects, knowledge, skills, in proper blocs and sequences and at the proper time. He must adjust to the teacher, to the class, and to the community in terms of his knowledge and skills. He must conform in those adjustments to the dictates of society, vocation, government, religion, and other ruling systems of behavior and thought.

The acquire-adjust-conform combination has seldom been so well exemplified as in the pre-1945 Japanese system of education and culture which began with bowing to the Emperor's portrait and ended with thought police. It is a matter for sober reflection that a very similar education could be initiated with flag idolatry and developed, through avoidance of disloyal acts, to a complete rejection of any ideas which might be held by subversive groups.

I say *could be*, since it is hard for us Americans to conceive of a situation in which our thoughts would be policed. Unconsciously we rely upon a type of mountaineering in our education to protect us in the free exercise of idiosyncrasy in thought, at least. We should ask ourselves, however, whether the official thought-control process is not already at work when a committee of the Congress through the newspapers accuses a government scientist of disloyalty, and then refuses for months to give him a hearing. How much freedom of thought, under such conditions, remains to government workers or to young men and women aspiring to be employed by the government?

Not long ago almost any student of American education would have said that thought policing by applying the doctrine of guilt through thought association would be impossible in the United States of America. Today he could not be so sure. The year 1949 marked the issuance of a document by the headquarters of the Supreme Commander for the Allied Powers in Japan in which American citizens were solemnly told that the history of a Soviet spy ring in Japan prior to World War II shows us that we cannot trust the loyalty of our closest friends or even relatives, and that persons who have sympathized with Communist causes, even though not themselves Communists, must be prevented from occupying security positions.

Upon that basis, of course, the Commander-in-Chief of the United States Armed Forces would be called by any Dixiecrat a very poor national security risk. He should not be given access even to restricted and much less to confidential or secret materials. He has proposed a civil-rights program for Negroes which the Communist Party supports. Every public-school man in the United States who believes in free and compulsory education is a poor security risk. Every Communist government in the world preaches the same doctrine. The president of the University of Maryland has been assailed by a local news sheet on the chief grounds that he is trying to give higher education to young men and women whose parents cannot afford to pay private college tuition fees. According to the guilt-by-association theory, the paper has an open-and-shut case against the president. Every Communist in Maryland agrees with him. So do many of the clergymen of the Roman Catholic Church, and the president might well be accused, therefore, of subservience to a foreign power, the Holy See.

These are not merely straws in the wind—they are more like haystacks in the cyclone. The loud-mouthed declaimer of the correct thought, the patrioteer who screams most passionately of loyalty while stealing from the taxpayers, the defender of the United States who often never bore arms for the United States but is quick to protect his country by accusing a dead man of treason with no grounds for the accusation except a love for headlines—these are signs of a culture passing in some parts under the tutelage of pedagogical plainsmen.

The defense against this drift towards pedagogical plainsmanship cannot be brought by arms, by law, or even by exhortation. It can be purchased only at the price of a mountaineering education of democratic power and scope.

The creed of the educational mountaineer provides that force to do democracy's work. It contains two main articles of faith. The first is that of equality of opportunity; the second is that of equality of efficiency.

To give equality of opportunity, the mountaineering educator starts with a maximum of understanding for every child. That means that every child will be studied as precisely and extensively as present techniques allow. The crippled, six-year-old colored girl of modest intellectual ability will get just as much understanding as research and practice can provide. The physically perfect six-year-old white boy of highest intellectual capacity will also get just as much understanding as research and practice can provide.

Why not give more understanding to the child with the higher ability?

It cannot be done. There is no more understanding available than the educational mountaineer gives to every one of his learners.

To give equality of efficiency, the educational mountaineer develops the crippled six-year-old's personality, let us say, by teaching her tap-dancing. She can move her right foot only by dragging it on the floor, but she can lift her left foot off the floor and move the toe and heel. She learns to tap-dance with her left foot.

"Tap-dancing a first-grade subject?" screams the plainsman. "If it's good for one child, it's good for *all of them*. Democracy demands that they all learn the multiplication tables. If democracy demands tap-dancing at all, it demands it for all."

The mountaineer says, "I am not teaching tap-dancing. I am teaching a shy child to be more confident. I am taking a tiny peak of ability and trying to make it a tower of idiosyncrasy by which one who may some day be a great woman in her own right can get her first secure moorings."

The educational mountaineer develops the six-year-old of high intellectual capacity by encouraging him to study osmosis.

"Osmosis in the first grade?" cries the plainsman. "Osmosis is a high-school subject. That's where we teach it for everybody in good democratic fashion."

But the mountaineer says again, "I am not teaching osmosis. I am teaching one who is a great genius to be in truth the great genius that he is."

Here I pause to point out the inescapable fact that the mountaineer must know how to teach tap-dancing and osmosis if he is going to use them as means of developing personalities and characters. In a reasonably long lifetime of observation of educational plainsmen and educational mountaineers in many kinds of schools and in many parts of the globe, I have seen no slightest evidence that those teachers who believe that education starts, proceeds, and ends with a developing individual have as a group any less erudition and command of subject matter than have those teachers who believe that education starts with a required curriculum and ends with mastery of a minimum essential. I have indeed seen evidence to indicate that a truly profound command of a field of knowledge inclines men toward the pedagogical peaks. How else can we account for the prevalence of mountaineers in the great graduate schools?

Whether the mountaineer is in the graduate school or in the first grade, whether he is educating citizens in the high school or officers in the Army, his answers to the double-barreled question raised earlier . . . are clear, concise, and unequivocal.

How much uniformity does this society need for safety?

It needs *only that uniformity which the achievements of its greatest goals require.* It demands security of life and health for its people. It demands wide opportunities for its people in work and play, in song and prayer. It must provide each individual with maximum aid to the development of his powers to contribute in every way possible to the great goals of his people.

Are there necessary restrictions on the individual's development? Of course there are. Should there be guidance, direction, in the building of his abilities? Of course there should be. The child with an idiosyncrasy of aggression cannot be permitted to develop it into an idiosyncrasy for brutality, mayhem, or murder. He must instead be helped to develop it into an idiosyncrasy for fighting disease through the practice of medicine, battling hunger by farming, breaking down isolation by blasting highways through mountains, or doing some other aggressive job commensurate with his pattern of abilities.

It requires just as much deviation, just as many uniquely developed peaks of ability, just as much idiosyncrasy as the attainment of its goals will allow and need. All societies are wasteful of the capacities of their people. That society which comes closest to developing every socially useful idiosyncrasy in every one of its members will make the greatest progress toward its goals.

The key decision on both the matter of minimum safety and the matter of maximum progress is this decision concerning the amount of caution needed to protect the society's goals and the amount of daring required to advance the society toward those goals.

Who makes that decision?

In a democracy, the people make it.

In this democracy, I have heart and faith that our people will not make the decision very wrong. This is because I believe they are a great people and a strong people, not just in population or in number of tons of steel they can produce annually, but in those measures of meaning which God Himself uses to gauge the tides of history. I think they will make educational room for themselves in the future according to their size and strength.

The Selection of Teacher Candidates

Continuous Selection of Professional Personnel

Some Assumptions About Selection in the Profession

The task of educating all the children of all the people in an increasingly complex world is difficult. The more successful public education in a democracy becomes, the more diverse the student population in terms of ability, background, interests, and needs. As a result, demands on the scope of knowledge, skills, and understandings of the teaching staff are also greatly increased.

Well-qualified personnel become imperative to sane survival. Teachers have major responsibility for developing trained man power for all the other professions and occupations essential to our culture. But above all, teachers must educate a citizenry that can live peaceably in a global community, and perhaps even be neighborly in the universe.

The right and responsibility of institutions preparing teachers and of the profession itself to select persons admitted to preparation for teaching and to its practice are based on several assumptions. One assumption is that each student has the right, not only to the amount and kind of education from which he can profit most, but to counseling, guidance, and teaching by persons qualified through selection and preparation for their positions.

A second assumption is that the individual being selected for the teaching profession has the right to guidance and counseling which will help him select that for which his capabilities and interests best suit him. Conversely, he should expect the selective process to prevent his entering a field for which by personality and ability he is unqualified and

"The Selection of Teacher Candidates (Excerpts from "New Horizons in Teacher Education and Professional Standards," Margaret Lindsey, Co-ordinator of article, *National Education Association Journal* [January, 1961], 56–58.)

in which his contribution to society is minimized and his individual satisfactions are jeopardized.

A third assumption is that students can be selected wisely both for teacher preparation and for admission to the profession, and that continued effective performance for retention in the profession can be satisfactorily evaluated.

Any selective program is subject to human fallibility, and subjective judgment may result in the exclusion of some individuals who would make good teachers and the inclusion of others who do not. Nevertheless, careful selection procedures minimize error and recognize the importance of professional service to society.

A major purpose of any professional program is to provide an adequate supply of adequately prepared practitioners for the field. There is considerable evidence that well-defined, consistently applied programs of identification, selective admission and retention contribute significantly to both the quality and quantity of the supply of teachers.

The relationship of the selective process to all aspects of professional preparation and performance is crucial. Certification of teachers, their placement and performance, their further preparation, and their self- and group-discipline are all dependent for effectiveness on the validity and continuing nature of the selective process.

Judicious efforts should be made to expand and extend selective admission and retention programs, from the point of identification of individuals through evaluation of their performance as continuing members of the profession. Criteria need to be developed through longitudinal studies and constantly evaluated and applied to all potential and practicing members of the profession, whether the position be that of kindergarten teacher or professor in a graduate school.

Some Difficulties in the Process of Selection

An impressive amount of investigation and research has been devoted to the study of specific criteria and means to be employed in selecting students for teacher education. Findings from the many studies of teacher characteristics and of factors related to teaching success or failure are leading to improved programs of selection. The accumulation of information from these studies suggests that a constellation of factors is important in teaching and that it is difficult to identify a factor that in isolation may be used as a critical index.

Attempts to identify factors that would aid in predicting teaching effectiveness or success in the general sense have led to little more than an appreciation of the complexity of the problem. This may be true because teaching effectiveness appears to be situational in the sense that the interaction of teacher, pupil, setting, and subject matter affect the success of the teacher from one situation to the next. It may be equally true because success and effectiveness are not easily defined and measured.

The fact that predicting success is difficult does not argue against all selection. There are personal factors that are widely accepted as desirable in teachers and that provide a basis for urging persons who possess them to enter teaching. Similarly, there are personal characteristics that are widely accepted by parents, by pupils, and by teachers as being undesirable.

Investigations conducted during the last two decades particularly seem to suggest that there are a few broad categories of qualities that must be possessed, at least at a minimum level. One such quality is intellectual ability. Another is communication skill. A third is physical health. Questions persist, however, on definitions of these qualities and on what is an acceptable minimum.

Perhaps the most commonly discussed of these broad categories is one variously labeled "emotional stability," "mental health," or "teaching personality." On its importance there is wide agreement among college staff engaged in preparing teachers. Samplings of their opinions have repeatedly shown a wide concern that personality factors be assessed as colleges select students for teacher preparation.

How personality is to be appraised is more difficult to establish. What is it? How is it observed and how can it be measured? At what point is appraisal to be attempted? Should selection focus on choosing the best applicants or on rejecting the unfit?

An increasing number of colleges have been seeking answers to these questions. Little is known about the personality characteristics of teachers that foster the educational development of pupils. Experience gained in a number of schools suggests that the most effective selection program results if attention to personality assessment is devoted to identifying those whose behavior is unacceptable.

Obviously unacceptable would be those persons whose behavior is so bizarre as to disrupt the work of a class. More likely to escape notice but equally ineffective as teachers, would be individuals who are insensitive to the thoughts and feelings of students and who are, therefore, unaware of what they as teachers might do or say at a particular moment to aid understanding or learning.

Persons may fail on this score for at least two reasons. They may be so set on dominating and controlling pupils that they become too rigid to respond to them. Others may be living in a small world of their own, apart from the class.

Yet another kind of person may be ineffective as a teacher because he has such great need to be liked by pupils that he is led to excesses in seeking favor. Not infrequent, too, is the charming but irresponsible individual whose commitment to others is so slight that he cannot be depended upon to perform the work of a teacher. These are but examples of kinds of behavior that those engaged in preparing teachers may regard as unacceptable.

The availability of personality inventories has led some colleges to experiment with these in the hope that they may predict teaching behavior. These instruments have not been particularly effective as screening devices. The most successful of these inventories were developed as aids to diagnosis rather than for purposes of prediction.

This does not condemn the use of personality inventories in college. Although it is inappropriate to eliminate an applicant on the basis of a score on an inventory, some of the instruments available may be used to supplement the observations relative to selection or as an aid in counseling.

Selection on the basis of personality characteristics must depend often on observations made after a student is admitted to college. The usual teacher education program provides important opportunities for such observation of students in college classes, on the campus, in laboratory experiences, including student teaching.

Many programs specify that there shall be continuing selection throughout the college years with careful review of each candidate at specified points, such as admission to student teaching. Information that is systematically collected about each student may be reviewed at such times.

Before a student is discontinued in his educational program, whether it be for personality reasons or for other difficulties, he should have an opportunity to discuss the matter with a representative of the college. In order that he may try to overcome the difficulty or find a more appropriate goal, it is also desirable that the college offer counseling assistance.

When questions are raised about continuing a student in teacher preparation, the college owes it to the student and to itself to conduct a study of the case through an established faculty committee. Committee action makes it more likely that college policy will be applied in a uniform manner to all cases, that capricious acts will be avoided, and that deliberate decisions based on studied facts will be made.

J. A. BATTLE

The Power of Man

I read a story on the sports page of a local newspaper the other week about a visit to our town of Minnesota Fats, the pool shark whom Jackie Gleason is supposed to have copied for his role in *The Hustler*. The paper carried Minnesota's picture, too, and if one can judge by his picture, Jackie Gleason did not have to go on a diet to copy him. The story mainly concerned Minnesota's pleasurable activities at lunch at the Riverboat Restaurant. The story left no doubt that he not only enjoys eating but is a champion in this field, too. But champion or not, I was not impressed, as hogs are also outstanding as eaters, until I read that Minnesota felt no twinges of conscience telling himself that he should not eat so much. According to the sports writer, Minnesota didn't say, "I know I shouldn't but I'll have a piece of that pie." Minnesota had several pieces of pie and did not say anything about whether he should not. His actions indicated that *he should*.

I usually don't like lunching with champion eaters but I'd surely like to go to lunch with Minnesota, not to watch him eat but to watch a big eater *not* wrestle with his conscience when and after he eats. I guess I have just had too many meals spoiled by having to watch grown men wrestle with their consciences and lose. From somewhere in the dim past I recall a little rhyme that may have a moral for unsuccessful conscience wrestlers. It was written by a talented soul who for a guess I'll say was Ogden Nash. As I remember it, the rhyme went something like this:

> The only people who should really sin
> Are the people who can sin with a grin,
> Because if sinning upsets you,
> Why, nothing at all is what it gets you.*

Eric Gill once said that it is a sin to eat inferior ice cream, and according to Walter Kerr, *New York Times* drama critic, he was serious when he said it. Kerr says further that if the statement shocks us or impresses us as the remark of a man given to silliness, it is partly because

* Ogden Nash, "Inter-Office Memorandum," *Verses from 1929 On.* Copyright 1935, by Ogden Nash. By permission of Little, Brown and Co.

we have ceased to believe in sin and partly because we have ceased to believe in ice cream. He says Mr. Gill was being strict about both. Mr. Kerr defines sin as, "A defect in the quality of an act, a deliberate failure to perform a natural act perfectly." To demonstrate self-control and integrity is "to perform a natural act perfectly" but to do otherwise is a defect. Sin is less than the situation requires. It keeps man from shaping his fate in a heroic style. Now Minnesota Fats may or may not sin by eating so heavily but as he eats he does not exhibit poor manners and an inability to act as he desires to act. Fortunately for his own pleasure and that of his dining companions, Minnesota is unlike so many other overeaters who spoil every meal by declaring again and again that they should not eat so much as they gorge themselves. Those who overeat without enjoying their food may be committing two sins instead of one, the first against the body and the second against the spirit of life.

Now we will leave the champion combination eater and pool player, Minnesota Fats, and go back to some speculation on what Mr. Gill meant by his statement that it is a sin to eat inferior ice cream. Hear one speculation and then you can speculate. The primary value of ice cream is not its food value but the pleasure it gives. The man who deliberately eats ice cream that displeases, for whatever reasons, is sinning according to Mr. Kerr's definition of sin, for as surely as "a lie denies the nature of truth" to "eat ice cream that displeases is to engage in an act which denies its own nature." While this discussion may seem to be only verbal sparring, it has an implication that is more far-reaching than eating inferior ice cream. One who eats inferior ice cream is not only denying the nature of ice cream but is supporting the popularly held assumption that what one dislikes is good for him and what one likes is bad for him. Plainly put, this means that something must be wrong with the human system of perceiving what is good and what is bad or else something must be wrong with the assumption. It is easier for me to believe that something is wrong with the assumption.

Many people are saying today that education is too important to be left to the educators and some are even saying that sin is too important to be left only to the sinners or only to those who are professionally qualified to preach against it. Educators have been taught to be rather timid in fields in which they hold no expertness, but, since they have that expertness in education, they should feel no timidity in moving against those who promote the assumption that what one dislikes is good for one since such promoters have moved into the educational domain with a vengeance. They are trying to spoil education, too, by insisting that students should not enjoy reading, writing, and reasoning. They are trying to impose on the school their belief that unless the young leave school with the same relief that they feel when leaving the dentist that their educational programs have gone soft. It is this type of thought that keeps the spirit of life from being used to improve education.

There is much confusion today as to the meaning of "the spirit of life." Recently I was talking to some teachers who had been attending a class here at the University of South Florida given by a visiting lecturer. They were in a state of delight about what they had gained from the lecturer. I asked them what they had learned that they did not know before. They hesitated but finally said that they were not sure of that, but they were very sure that they would be much better teachers for having taken the course because their professor put "a new spirit into our lives." These teachers knew the importance of the spirit of life. But when I asked them if they thought that they had enjoyed an intellectual experience in the class, they seemed most puzzled by the question. One of them asked, "Can one *enjoy* an intellectual experience?"

Most Americans seem to believe that intellectual experiences are not to be enjoyed, for the word "intellectual" to thm has a funereal connotation. To them thought does not seem a pleasure and cannot add to the spirit of life. Possibly because it seems so unpleasant to think about poverty, the bomb, and the computer, most American citizens today are leaving the solutions of the first two problems to LBJ and the latter to IBM. Yet there would probably be few things in life more satisfying, if not more pleasant, than to think well enough to determine how to keep the bomb from ending life on earth and, if life does continue, how to utilize the computer as a humanizing rather than a dehumanizing device.

Man's most distinctive feature is his ability to think. What man needs most today is a faith in his ability to so improve in his thinking process that he can control himself and his world. But as long as he believes thought to be unpleasant he will shun it. If man is to improve his thought processes he has to realize that while thinking is difficult it can be both significant and pleasant. Overcoming difficulties can be the most pleasant of experiences.

Although thinking is a self-directed process this does not mean that a person is free to think as he pleases. To think at all one must follow the dictates of the facts of the situation and of reason. One may believe that thinking as he pleases without regard to facts and reason will give him pleasure but, in the first place, what he is doing is not thinking and, in the second place, what he is doing is almost sure to bring misery instead of pleasure.

The slogan, "think young" is also a contradiction in terms. The philosophy of pleasure based on this slogan assures that its advocates will remain in a perpetual state of immaturity and never learn to think. Because he has observed in modern society so much immaturity Eric Hoffer, author of *The True Believer*, predicts in his latest book, *The Temper of Our Times*, that there is real reason to fear the advent soon of "a population juvenilized and primitized." Unless a cure is found for the prevailing "think young" syndrome, the people of the world are likely to be soon brainwashed into becoming a vast juvenile generation in which the older generation imitates instead of leading the young. The cure is not to be found in preachments against this syndrome, but in helping the young to gain the power to think. Then the slogan will have no appeal.

Man today, instead of feeling he is master of his fate, has so little faith that he can control himself or his own inventions such as nuclear energy and the computer that he lives in cringing fear that if the bomb doesn't destroy him the computer will destroy his purpose in living. Yet man's salvation and the salvation of his world depend upon his no longer being a servile, nonthinking coward too paralyzed to act at all except to seek shallow and fleeting pleasures to help him forget reality, but instead becoming one who thinks clearly and then acts courageously. He has to have faith in himself so to think and act.

Modern man needs the same faith in the power of man as was held by the early Greeks. Sophocles expressed this faith of his heroic race through the Theban Elders in *Antigone:*

> Of all the wonders beneath the Sun
> The most wonderful is Man
> He weareth Earth unweariedly
> He hath taught himself Speech
> And wind-swift Thought
> Only from Death doth he call for aid in vain.

The ages in history that have been great have had at least one element in common. In great ages man has felt as did the psalmist that he is only "a little lower than the angels." If the coming age is to be a great one, man will have to regain such a faith in himself. He must trust that once again he can teach himself the "wind-swift Thought" that will give him the power needed to control himself and his universe.